T0268896

A Lay Minister's Guide to
The Book of Common Prayer

Clifford W. Atkinson

MOREHOUSE PUBLISHING
H A R R I S B U R G , P A

Morehouse Publishing
P.O. Box 1321
Harrisburg, PA 17105

ISBN: 978-0-8192-1454-6

Library of Congress Cataloging-in-Publication Data

Atkinson, Clifford W.
  A lay minister's guide to the Book of common prayer/Clifford
W. Atkinson.
       p.   cm.
  Rev. ed. of: A lay reader's guide to the Book of common prayer. © 1977
  Bibliography: p.
  1. Lay ministry—Episcopal Church. 2. Episcopal Church. Book of
common prayer (1979). I. Atkinson, Clifford W. Lay reader's guide to the
Book of common prayer. II. Episcopal Church. Book of common prayer
(1979) III. Title.
  BX5968.A85 1988
  246'.03—dc19   88-5147
                                                              CIP

Printed in the United States of America

03 02 01   10 9 8 7 6 5

A NOTE ON NAMES

Earlier versions of this book have been called *The Lay Reader's Guide to the Book of Common Prayer.* In content and format, it was designed to be used by those who were licensed to be responsible for worship in a congregation that did not have the services of the ordained clergy on a regular basis.

The canon governing lay ministry and liturgy was changed, however. The new governances reflect the sweeping changes in worship patterns that began with what is called "the liturgical revival" and which culminated in the adoption of the present *Book of Common Prayer* in 1979. The assumption of the BCP now is that all liturgy is a shared responsibility among the ministry of the Church, lay and ordained.

This version of the *Guide* is meant to reflect the new canon and to respond to the increasing use of lay leaders, licensed and unlicensed, in Sunday worship. Since many lay responsibilities are not those of a "lay reader," but do require direction, it seemed appropriate to change the name of this volume in order more faithfully to reflect its current contents.

TABLE OF CONTENTS

INTRODUCTION

Within the life of the Church, from the beginning, there has been a variety of ministries. Each, according to St. Paul, is a specific gift of the Holy Spirit. A desire to fulfill any of these ministries is a result of what theologians call "prevenient grace." The Holy Spirit moves us to serve, before we can recognize Who it is that is urging us. However we recognize the source of our desire to serve, or in whatever words we express it, the desire is derived from the Holy Spirit, and the fulfillment of the desire, accredited by the Church, is ministry.

The roots of our worship go deep into Old Testament history. The expression of our corporate responsibility to God, which the People of God express as liturgy, is derived, not only from the experience of the people of the New Covenant, but from the longer experience of our brothers and sisters of the Old Covenant. Nowhere is this clearer than in the ministry.

In the Israel of our Lord's time, there were two levels upon which worship was carried out: the Altar and the Book. In the Temple there were daily sacrifices. The great pilgrim feasts, required by the Old Testament law, were celebrated in the Temple, at the altar. The ministry of the altar was a priestly ministry, centering upon sacrifice. The ministry of the Word was carried on daily in the synagogues, where learned men, who were not priests, read the Word, taught the Word, praised God for his presence in Israel, and offered intercession and thanksgiving for the people. As the ministry of the altar was priestly, so the ministry of the Word was a lay ministry.

In Christian worship, we have adapted the same general pattern. The sacrificial ministry of the altar, to which is given the power to bless and to forgive, is a priestly ministry. Unlike the priestly ministry of the Old Covenant, the Christian priesthood derives from vocation, not inheritance. Like the priesthood of the Old Covenant, however, it accepts and presents the offerings of the people, it presents the sacrifice acceptable to God, it performs the rituals through which the benefits of the atonement are made available to the People of God; it pronounces blessing in God's name.

The Word and its proclamation is central to Christian worship, whether in the Word of God in the Eucharist or in the Daily Office. The ministry of that Word in the Christian worship tradition is largely a lay responsibility. Hence, the rubric on p. 13 of the BCP states that "in all services, the entire Christian assembly participates in such a way that the members of each order within the Church, lay persons, bishops, priests, and deacons, fulfill the functions proper to their respective orders, as set forth in the rubrical directions for each service." The reading of the Daily Office is traditionally a ministry shared by the whole Christian assembly. The role of the lay order in the Eucharist is stated in the rubrics preceding the liturgy (pp. 332 and 354): "Lay persons appointed by the celebrant should normally be assigned the reading of the lessons which precede the gospel, and may lead the Prayers of the People"

In order to provide guidelines and promote the "decency and order" in worship of which St. Paul speaks in 1 Corinthians, certain canonical and rubrical directives have been provided (see Appendix IV). The first thing to note in studying these canons is the order of authority. The rubrics of the BCP are the first authority. "In every respect, the person licensed shall conform to the requirements and limitations set forth in the rubrics and other directions of the Book of Common Prayer."[1] The second level of authority is the bishop of the diocese in which the several lay ministries are performed. "The person licensed shall conform to the directions of the Bishop."[2] The third level of authority is "the Member of the Clergy in charge of the Congregation." It is the person with that authority who determines the particularity of dress, order of service, and the sermons or homilies to be read, as long as the rubrics of the Prayer Book and rules of the bishop have been conformed to.[3]

The first clear implication of the line of authority is underlined in Section 1(a) of Title III, Canon 3. The eligibility requirements for licensure to any specialized lay liturgical ministry are made clear: one must be a confirmed adult communicant in good standing. These are technical terms defined in Title I, Canon 17.

This canon defines an *adult communicant* as one who is sixteen or over and has received communion three times in the preceding year.[4] A *communicant in good standing,* however, is one "who for the previous year [has] been faithful in corporate worship, unless for good cause prevented, and [has] been faithful in working, praying and giving for the spread of the Kingdom of God...."[5] One becomes a confirmed person in one of several ways: One can be baptized as an adult and receive the laying on of hands; one can be baptized as an adult and at some later date reaffirm one's vows and receive the laying on of hands; one can receive the laying on of hands from a bishop in apostolic succession in another communion and be received by a bishop of this communion; one can be baptized as an infant and at some later time receive the laying on of hands by a bishop.[6]

To recapitulate: in order to be licensed to a special lay liturgical ministry, one needs to be sixteen or over, have been confirmed (or its equivalent), receive sacrament at least three times yearly, and attend worship regularly, as well as work, pray, and give for the spread of God's Kingdom. If one conforms to these standards, then one may apply for a license as lay reader, pastoral leader, lay preacher, catechist, or lay eucharistic minister. The rules regarding selection and requirements for training rest with the diocesan bishop.[7] For that reason, no general rule can be laid down beyond those of the Canon 17 itself.

An area left gray is the role of a lay person who reads a lesson but does not conduct worship, read homilies, or the like. In many dioceses, the choice of persons to fill this role is left to the parish priest, with no license required. If one wishes to perform that task, it would be well to ascertain diocesan guidelines. The same is true for persons who lead the Prayers of the People. It is not clear if that is "conducting worship."

[1] Title III, Canon 3, Sec. 2d.
[2] *Ibid.*
[3] *Ibid.*
[4] Title I, Canon 17, Sec. 2 (a) and (b).
[5] *Ibid.*, Sec. 3.
[6] *Ibid.*, Sec. 1 (d).
[7] Title III, Canon 3, Sec. 1(a).

LAY PARTICIPATION IN THE MINISTRY OF THE WORD

One technical term for the part of the eucharist preceding the Offertory is *synaxis*. It is an important word, because it comes from the same Greek word as "synagogue," reminding us of the source of the ministry of the Word. The synaxis and the Daily Office (Morning or Evening Prayer) come from the same source and share a basic common format: reading of lessons from scripture, a statement of faith, and prayers. Central to a ministry of the Word is the liturgical year, which determines what lessons will be read, what emphasis the service will take. Like the ministry of the Word itself, the pivot of the year is Jewish in origin.

In order to understand the nature of the ministry of the Word, it is important, obviously, to study the structure of the liturgical (Christian) year.

The Liturgical Year

Because the BCP places particular emphasis on the Christian year, it is appropriate to review its nature.

There is a fairly detailed discussion of the Calendar on pp. 15-18 of the BCP. It starts with the statement: The Church Year consists of two cycles of feasts and holy days: one is dependent upon the movable date of the Sunday of the Resurrection or Easter Day; the other, upon the fixed date of December 25, the feast of our Lord's Nativity or Christmas Day" (BCP, p. 15). Since these two cycles, with their seasons of preparation, take up only about half of the year's Sundays, and since those

1

two festal cycles are irregularly and movably placed, the rest of the Sundays must come in two groups of uneven and variable length. There are, then, two classes of Sundays: those associated with the Nativity and Paschal Cycles, which we shall, for want of a better term, call "special" Sundays; those which separate those cycles, which we shall simply call "green" Sundays, after the color used on the altar. The year, then, looks like this:

> The Nativity Cycle (Advent through the Feast of the Epiphany)
> The Feast of the Baptism of our Lord and the other Sundays after Epiphany
> The Paschal Cycle (Ash Wednesday through Pentecost)
> Trinity Sunday and the other Sundays after Pentecost

From this are derived six seasons (cf. BCP p. 31ff.):

> Advent
> Christmas and associated feasts
> Epiphany
> Lent and Holy Week
> Easter season
> Sundays after Pentecost

Each of these seasons has its own emphasis. In Advent, we are concerned with the preparation for both the first coming of the Messiah, in Bethlehem, and the second coming of the Messiah, as Judge, at the end of all things. (Some of the latter emphasis has been shifted to the Sundays just before Advent, but the thrust remains, nonetheless.) The mood is one of anticipation, a mixture of joy and dread. A careful reading of the Advent hymns in the Hymnal, as well as hymns 462, 598 and 640 will help give a good sense of the season.

The Christmas emphasis is, of course, on the events and the theology surrounding the birth of Jesus. The season proper consists of the twelve days from Christmas to Epiphany. The former concentrates upon the events of our Lord's birth as they are told in Saint Luke's Gospel, the latter on the events as they are recorded in Saint Matthew's Gospel.

The Christian Year

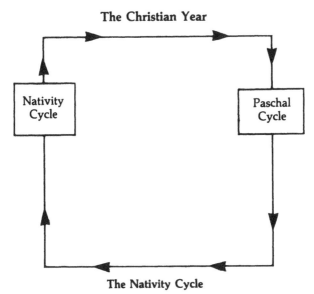

The Nativity Cycle

The Four Sundays in Advent

Christmas and its associated feasts

The Feast of the Nativity	25 December
The Feast of St. Stephen	26 December
The Feast of St. John	27 December
The Feast of the Holy Innocents	28 December
The Feast of the Holy Name	1 January

The Epiphany   6 January

The Feast of the Baptism of our Lord   Sunday after the Epiphany

The Paschal Cycle

The forty days and six Sundays in Lent

Easter and its associated feast
The Feast of the Ascension on the fortieth day of Easter

Pentecost on the fiftieth day of Easter and its associated feast
The Feast of the Trinity   First Sunday after Pentecost

Within the cycle of events that might be characterized as "the life of Jesus from shepherds to wise men," there are four other events that are regularly kept. On the day after Christmas, the Feast of Saint Stephen, the first martyr, is observed. Traditionally, he is referred to as a martyr by will and deed, since he wished for martyrdom and received it. On the next day, we commemorate Saint John the Evangelist. He is referred to as a martyr by will but not by deed because, in the tradition it is said that he wished to be a martyr, like the rest of the apostles, but that he was the only one to die a natural death. On the day after that, we keep the Feast of the Holy Innocents, commemorating the Herod's slaughter of the boys under two. They are referred to as martyrs by deed, but not by will because they bore witness to Jesus by their deaths, although they did not will to do so. Taken with the witness of the shepherds, these three witnesses (the word "martyr" means witness) lead up to the Feast of the Epiphany.

On the Epiphany we celebrate the coming of the wise men to the cradle. In the tradition, the Magi came from the three non-semitic races known to the medieval world. Many traditional creche sets, therefore, show the Magi as white, black, and yellow. The tradition says that God called the Magi so that the witness to Jesus could be spread throughout the world.

In addition to the three holy days immediately following the Feast of the Nativity, on its octave we keep the Feast of the Holy Name, which reminds us that the whole event to which we are witnessing is the event that leads to our salvation. As the Book of Acts reminds us, "For there is salvation in no one else, since no other name under the heaven is given to humanity through which we can be saved." (Acts 4:12).

The Sunday after the Feast of the Epiphany (which is always January 6), we keep the Feast of the Baptism of our Lord. This is God's witness to Jesus as Messiah. At the baptism, the Holy

Spirit personally bore witness that Jesus is, indeed, the "beloved son."

The Epiphany season, which begins with the feast itself, continues after the Feast of the Baptism of our Lord as a green season. Its length is determined by the date of the Feast of the Resurrection. It is to be noted that there is a fixed collect and set of lections that is used for the Last Sunday after Epiphany, regardless of the length of the season. The green portion of the season moves in tone from a reflection of the concern for witness that marked its beginning toward a preparation for the coming season of Lent. The concern of the collects shifts, the lessons deal less immediately with the manifestation of Christ. The lections for the Last Sunday after the Epiphany always include the story of the transfiguration, which was our Lord's own preparation for his final journey to Jerusalem and a foretaste of the glory that would succeed His crucifixion and resurrection. The collect reflects the theme fully. The significance of the day is underlined by the fact that it is the last occasion on which one may use either the *Gloria in excelsis* or an alleluia until the Easter Vigil. Hymns 122 and 123 in the Hymnal 1982 stress both the fact of the last use of alleluia, and give a reason for it. The rule for use of the Gloria is found in a rubric on p. 406 of the BCP.

The Paschal Cycle begins with the preparatory season of Lent. It is a season of forty weekdays and six Sundays. The purpose and thrust of the season is best described by the BCP itself. In one of the proper prefaces for Lent, it says: "You bid your faithful people cleanse their hearts, and prepare with joy for the Pascal feast; that, fervent in prayer and in works of mercy, and renewed by your Word and Sacrament, they may come to the fullness of grace which you have prepared for those who love you." (BCP, p. 379, cf. p. 346) In the service for Ash Wednesday, the specifics of the season are more fully spelled out. "I invite you, therefore, in the name of the Church, to the observance of a holy Lent, by self-examination and repentance; by prayer, fasting, and self-denial; and by reading and meditating on God's holy Word. . . ."

Greater clarity is given to self-examination and repentance in the Exhortation, which reads: "Examine your lives and conduct by the rule of God's commandments, that you may perceive wherein you have offended in what you have done or left undone, whether in thought, word, or deed. And acknowledge your sins before Almighty God, with full purpose of amendment of life, being ready to make restitution for all injuries and wrongs done by you to others; and also being ready to forgive those who have offended you, in order that you yourselves may be forgiven." (BCP, p. 317)

All of Lent points toward Holy Week and the Feast of the Resurrection. The Calendar on p. 31 of the BCP lists Holy Week as a special subseason. It begins with Palm Sunday, whose lessons contrast sharply the joy with which Jesus was received into Jerusalem and the cries of the crowd that he be crucified. Note that there is a special liturgy of Palms starting on p. 270 that may be used by a lay reader in the absence of a priest or deacon. The same is true for the special Good Friday liturgy that begins on p. 276. In the days between Palm Sunday and Good Friday, the lessons trace the activities of our Lord in that climactic week of his life.

The paschal season of the "Great Fifty Days" extends from the first Easter service through Pentecost. Pentecost is the Greek name for the Jewish Feast of Weeks. It is a Sabbath of Sabbaths or fifty days (counting both ends in) from Passover. It was on this feast that the Holy Spirit was poured out on the apostles. Thus, the Church counts a Sabbath of Sabbaths from the Christian Passover to the Christian Pentecost. It is the resurrection of Christ that marks the Christian Passover. Because this took place on "the first day of the week," our Passover is always Sunday, and every Sunday is a recollection of Christ's resurrection (cf. the Sunday collects in the Offices). The connection between Passover and Easter, however, has always been strong. There was even a small group of Christians, called Quartodecimans, (or "fourteeners"), who early in the life of the Church celebrated the Christian Passover on the Jewish date, Nisan 14. Although their logic in keeping the close connection between Passover and Easter was strong, the Church's emphasis on celebrating the first day of the week was stronger, and the sect disappeared. The adjective "paschal," by which we describe the resurrection festivities, derives from the Greek word for Passover, *pascha.* This is a transliteration of the Hebrew word for Passover, *pesach.* The early part of the season reflects the events surrounding the resurrection itself. Then, it moves to the contemplation of the meaning of the event. Finally it prepares, first for the ascension of Jesus to the Father, and then for the outpouring of the Spirit upon the Church at Pentecost. The tone of the season is joyful throughout.

The Feast of the Trinity, like that of the Baptism of our Lord, witnesses to the preceding festal season. As a feast, it is kept in white. It also starts the green season to follow. While the Feast of the Baptism of our Lord expresses the notion of witness to the preceding cycle, it is still a part of the Sundays after the Epiphany that follow. In the same way, the Feast of the Trinity is the summary of God's self-revelation. God showed himself both through the incarnate life of Jesus and through the outpouring of the Spirit. In addition, it is the First Sunday after Pentecost, the first of many to come.

The green season after Pentecost is the longest of the seasons and the least formal. Because the Church lives in the Spirit, is guided by the Spirit, is the instrument of the Spirit, it is appropriate that the longest season be a regular reminder of that relationship. The season after Pentecost is the season of that Spirit in whom we live, move, serve, and love.

In addition to the regular seasons, the Church commemorates various events in the life of our Lord and various saints and worthies of our past. If major commemorations occur on a Sunday that is not green, they are transferred to an open weekday. If, however, one of them occurs on a green Sunday that is neither the first nor the last Sunday of the green season, the commemoration may be kept on the Sunday.

This presents one with a choice. There are several things to be taken into consideration when making the decision. On the one hand, every Sunday is a commemoration of the resurrection of our Lord, and that consideration can never be lost. In addition, some disruption of the flow of the course readings would occur if the saint's day were to be observed. On the other hand, unless one's parish has regular and well attended weekday eucharists, it is unlikely that many in the congregation will have the opportunity to commemorate the saints, except at All Saints. Many of the prayers in the BCP include commemorations of the saints to remind us of our unity with those who have preceded us in the life of faith.

In the long run, one must decide on the basis of one's own parish, its customs, practices, and needs.

(*N.B.* All Saints Day, observed on November 1, may always be celebrated on the following Sunday).

The seasons themselves, however, take much of their shape from the lectionary, to which we now turn.

The Structure of the Lectionary

There are two lectionaries in the BCP. One is for use with the daily recitation of the Offices. The other is for use at the principal service of the Sunday, regardless of whether that service is an Office or a Eucharist, ". . . except when the same congregation attends two or more services" (BCP, p. 888). The rubrics for the Sunday lectionary are on p. 888 of the BCP and should be read with care. If there is reason to use the other lectionary, its rubrics are on p. 934. The one rubric of particular significance for anyone planning to read an office is the one that states, "When more than one Reading is used at an Office, the first is always from the Old Testament (or the Apocrypha)" (BCP, p. 934).

Each Sunday is provided with three lessons. One is from the Old Testament or Apocrypha. One is from the Epistles, Acts, or Revelation. One is from the Gospels. As the rubric above noted, unless one plans to read an Office with only one lesson, the first must be from the Old Testament or Apocrypha. As will be noted later, it is possible to use all three lessons. Indeed, there are occasions upon which it is preferable to read all three lessons. But if one must choose between the last two options, the selection is made easier if one is aware of the pattern in which the lessons are laid out.

As we noted above, there are two kinds of seasons in the Christian Year: green seasons and special seasons. The distinction is particularly important as regards the lectionary. Since over half of the Sundays in any given year are green, they tend to provide the pattern for the rest. The lections "for the principal morning service" are laid out in three cycles simply labled A, B, and C. The rubrics on p. 888 give the rules for determining the lectionary year. Cycle A is the year in which Saint Matthew's Gospel is the normative reading for the green Sundays. Saint Mark is read in B and Saint Luke in C.

On green Sundays, beginning with the Second Sunday after the Epiphany, and continuing in the Sundays after Pentecost, the Gospel for the year is read "in course," that is, in roughly continuous order, from the beginning.

On green Sundays, the epistle (middle) selection is also a course reading. Over the three-year cycle, most of the epistles are read. Since there are two simultaneous course readings provided, the relationship between the two New Testament readings is accidental. The Old Testament reading, on the other hand, is usually chosen to match the gospel. It may, however, on occasion be chosen to match the epistle. The relationship between the first lesson and the second is usually accidental. The relationship between the first and third is often deliberate. In Lent, however, the Old Testament lesson relates to neither of the other lessons. The stories are chosen as a retelling of the history of salvation. The considerations that one must take into account when deciding which lessons to use will be discussed later.

Since there are a varying number of Sundays after Pentecost, there usually are "extras." In the BCP, the propers for these "extra" Sundays are at the beginning of the long green season. To simplify things, each week's proper is numbered, the date of the nearest Sunday is given, and a calendar that provides the proper number for the Second Sunday after Pentecost is given on p. 884f.

In special seasons, the lesson choice is a function of the nature and role of the season itself. Readings are not necessarily in course. For this reason there is a closer integration among the three readings. All three tend to be mutually supportive and expressive of the season or feast. Usually, the gospel lesson is from Saint John.

Reading Aloud: Techniques and Content

Whether one is responsible for reading a whole Office or for lessons within the Office or the Eucharist, appropriate reading skills and awareness of the nature of the material one is to read are extremely important. There are significant differences between "being able to read" and reading publicly. There are at least three things to be concerned about in the actual practice of public reading: production, pace, and emphasis.

There are several basic rules to tone production and projection. They all begin with the fact that a vocal tone is produced by a column of air coming from the lungs and causing the voice box to vibrate. If that column of air is weak or irregular, the sound cannot be strong. For the column of air to be strong and regular, it must be supported. This support comes from the diaphragm, that band of muscles below the lungs that provide the muscular undergirding for the lungs. For the diaphragm to do any good at all, one must be standing erect, so that the muscles can "pull in the stomach." Erect posture and diaphragm support are the first essentials to proper tone production.

The second essential is adequate quantities of air. This requires deep breathing. Such deep breathing is easy and natural when one's posture is correct. One deep breath between major pauses, with smaller, "catch breaths" at natural breaks in the verbal line should keep adequate support under one's tone. Try never to feel short of breath toward the end of a sentence. If that happens, try one or more of several simple things. Try reading aloud more frequently in private. Part of the problem may be shallow breathing brought on by a touch of stage fright. Practice produces ease. Try standing erect, with the diaphragm tight. Take a deep breath and count slowly and aloud. See how many numbers it takes before there is too little breath to go on. If that is done several times a day, it will inevitably build up lung capacity and breath control.

Another major element in tone production is pitch. The higher the pitch of the voice, the more air is needed to keep the voice box vibrating, since the vibrations must be faster. The lower the pitch, the more support the column of air needs, because it is being released more slowly. A medium pitch within the normal range will use the air supply the most efficiently. It is easiest to use one's normal speaking pitch. It is the most comfortable, and the one to which one's tone-production equipment is most habituated.

For speaking purposes, consider a word to be made up of vowel sounds that are cut off and divided by consonants. The sounds that carry and are heard are the vowels. The sounds that distinguish one vowel from another and make the word intelligible are the consonants. To make the word audible, therefore, the vowels must project clearly. To make the word intelligible, the consonants must be crisp and distinguishable.

Projecting a vowel sound is primarily a question of placement. The further forward in the head and the more rounded the lips during the production of the vowel sound, the more clearly it will project. For example, pronounce "alleluia," with all its vowels; first with one's lips nearly in a smiling position. Listen to the "a" sound. Then produce just that "a." Continue to make that sound while moving the lips more nearly into a circle. Listen for the difference in the "a" sound as it is transformed by the lip movement. Then try projecting several of the possible "a" sounds that have been produced, speaking as loudly as possible. The rounder the lips, the further the projection. A reading tone should be as round as the proper pronunciation of the words will allow.

For speaking purposes, consonants serve three purposes: they initiate words; they divide syllables; they end words and separate them from their neighbors. Most consonants, as long as they are pronounced clearly, provide a minimum of difficulty. Some, however, especially as initiating or terminal consonants, need to be watched carefully. These are the "sharp" consonants: b, c/k, d, p, t. If not pronounced with care, they tend to disappear.

The larger the building, or the greater its capacity for echo, the more important it is to be sure that the consonants really do divide words. Words run together in a large building become unintelligible. For this reason, carefully pronounced consonants are essential.

As a general rule, all public reading should be slower than normal speech patterns, unless those patterns are unusually slow. The auditor is hearing language and ideas that are not "everyday" in nature or content. They are, moreover, words of particular importance. It is to be hoped that those listening are listening carefully. Careful listening is aided by deliberately paced reading. That is a function of carefully projected vowels and crisp, cleanly pronounced consonants.

Until one is sure of one's pace in reading, it might be well to have someone else listen to a passage being read, and report at what pace the language was most easily heard. Then, practice at the pace until it becomes second nature.

There are several kinds of literature in the Bible, and it is easier to read aloud if one has a basic understanding of the particulars of each. Two of the more important kinds of writing in the Bible are poetry and narrative. We will return to each later, because each provides its own challenge. The epistles and some sections of the Old Testament are neither narrative nor poetry. In them, ideas are communicated with which we are not entirely familiar in language styles that are now out of common use. To communicate these ideas clearly, it is important to emphasize the words in such a way that the meaning of the language becomes clear to the listener. To do that, one must understand the nature of the sentence and the role that its various component parts play.

The proper emphasis on the various words within a sentence is derived from the role that the individual words and phrases play within the structure of the sentence. It is particularly important to recognize this when dealing with the older forms, where the structure of the sentence is more apt to be unfamiliar to contemporary ears. If one can recognize how the various parts interrelate, however, reading with appropriate emphasis becomes easier.

No matter how long or complicated a sentence becomes, it has three benchmarks to which everything must relate: the subject, the verb and the complement. It is probably easiest to start out by looking for the person, pronoun (I, you, he, she, it, we, they) or thing who does whatever is done in the sentence. The subject often is very near the beginning of the sentence. When that is found, the word that describes what that subject does, or some form of the verb "to be" can be found. Then the person, pronoun, or thing to whom this action is done can be found. If the verb is some form of "to be," then look for a person, pronoun, or thing which is the same as the subject. In a sentence, the verb "to be" acts as an equal sign. Everything else in the sentence must, in one way or another, further define, describe, or delineate the subject, the verb, or the complement. In many cases, particularly in the older forms, this additional material is interspersed among the three basic parts of the sentence. That is less true in contemporary rites and translations. It is this complex separation that, in fact, gives the "churchy" flavor to the older forms. Such a style was the literary norm of the period and was based upon Greek and Latin models.

In some cases, if the action of the sentence is not direct (or active), but indirect (passive), there will be no direct object. For example, an active verb would occur in a sentence that went, "God helped me." In a sentence, "I was helped by God," the verb is passive, and there is no direct object. The latter is less usual, however.

In sum, then, look for the subject and the verb. Unless the latter is "to be" or passive, look for the object. If it is "to be," look for the complement that is the same as the subject. If it is passive, look for the agent of the action, which will serve the purpose of making a complete thought. Then try to find what parts of the sentence further define each. When that is done, the structure of the sentence will be clear. It is then possible to emphasize the main words most and relate the rest to each other by appropriate tone of voice.

There are several common pitfalls in public reading. One common one is to emphasize the preposition in a prepositional phrase. They are those small words like to, for, after, and among, which, with a noun, tend to define time or place. They are always followed by a noun. Only in the rarest of circumstances is the preposition emphasized. It is always the noun which receives the emphasis. Yet, far too often, one hears the reading the other way.

In the scriptures there is an abnormally large number of "ands." Quite often one finds these, too, being emphasized. In classical times, punctuation had not been invented, so the word "and" was ordinarily used much as we would use a comma nowadays. Since sentences tended to be longer and more complex than modern style calls for, the conjunction "and" is extremely common. It is also of less importance than it is in contemporary writing.

Most of the recent translations of the Old Testament print the poetry in poetic form. This clarifies the fact that it is poetry and makes it easier to read. A note on Hebrew prosody might be helpful here. Unlike much English poetry, Hebrew poetry neither rhymes nor scans. Its basis was the balance of two lines that said the same thing in different and complementary ways. The famous "Christmas prophecy" from Isaiah 9:2 is a good example:

> The people who walked in darkness have seen a great light:
> light has dawned upon them, dwellers in a land dark as death.

There are numerous variations on the basic pattern, too technical for our purposes and discussion. One may, at times, find several verses interrelated in a similar fashion, making a longer whole. But, when reading over a poetic passage from the Old Testament, the first thing to do is to look for the couplets so that they can be read as a unit with appropriate emphasis and then related to the couplets preceding and following to strengthen the meaning of the whole. In reading this literature, keep the evocative nature of language in mind, thus remembering that the repetition is designed, at least in part, as a way of increasing and reinforcing the number of personal experiences and memories that can be recalled to underline the meaning of the passage. The structure is essential to the content and needs to be made clear in the reading— (cf. p. 583, BCP). In some of the longer and more complex passages, however, even an experienced grammarian may have some difficulty in assigning appropriate words to subject, verb, or complement.

Two other techniques may also be helpful. One is what in some other disciplines is called "nesting." This describes the style in which ancient writers very often expressed themselves. The reason is clearer when one realizes that neither punctuation nor paragraphing were in use, so that the grammar itself had to define the limits of the sentence. In nesting, a thought begins and is interrupted by a related thought before it is completed. This insertion itself may be interrupted in the same way. Only the final idea of each nested sentence is complete in itself. Each successive partial idea is completed in reverse order, until the first idea is completed in the last phrase.

The following example from Romans 4:16f. will illustrate the style:

> **That is why it depends on faith,** *(in order that the promise may rest on grace and be guaranteed to all Abraham's descendants—* {*not only to adherents of the law but also to those who share the faith of Abraham*}, *for he is the father of us all, as it is written, "I have made you the father of many nations")*—**in the presence of the God in whom Abraham believed, who gives life to the dead and calls into existence the things that do not exist.**

If one comes across a long complicated sentence, it is a good idea to see if the first phrase is completed by the final phrase. If it is, the sentence is most probably nested, and one can go through and discover the various elements of the sentence, even create a copy to use at the lectern that will give clues for reading the passage intelligibly. The following is a passage from Phil. 3:8f. on which to practice:

> For his sake I have suffered the loss of all things, and count them as refuse, in order that I may gain Christ and be found in him, not having a righteousness of my own, based on law, but that which is through faith in Christ, the righteousness from God that depends on faith; that I may know him and the power of his resurrection, and may share his sufferings, becoming like him in his death, that if possible I may attain the resurrection from the dead.

In translations later than the Authorized Version, there has been a tendency to divide the nested sentences into several sentences, making the necessary grammatical adjustments. In some cases, however, the resulting sentences are still long, and the various subordinate members are less clearly defined. One way to deal with a complex sentence is to create "sense lines," putting the most important ideas at the margin and indenting secondary ideas, so that the sentence makes visual sense before trying to read it. Here is an example of a "sense line," using Romans 8:15b-17:

> When we cry, "Abba! Father!"
>   it is the Spirit himself
>   bearing witness with our spirit that
> we are children of God,
>   and if children, then heirs,
>   heirs of God
>   and fellow heirs with Christ,
> provided we suffer with him
>   in order that we may also be glorified with him.

One of the classic cases of nesting occurs in Ephesians 3:1-8, in the passage used as the epistle on Epiphany. In the Authorized Version, all eight verses are contained in one sentence. In the Revised Standard Version, this is increased to three sentences and part of two paragraphs. In the New English Bible, four sentences are used to translate the same passage. A careful reading of all three versions (as well as others) may give helpful insight into how to read any complex passages.

The following is a practice text for sense-line reading, using 2 Peter 1:20-21:

> First of all you must understand this, that no prophecy of scripture is a matter of one's own interpretation, because no prophecy ever came by the impulse of man, but men moved by the Holy Spirit spoke from God.

One of the most common literary forms in the Bible is narrative—the telling of stories. Both testaments abound in stories, and much of God's communication to us is made by letting us see others in situations similar to ours, so that we can see how God responded and trim our own actions accordingly. A classic example occurs in 2 Samuel 11:26-12:14. Many, if not most of the stories depend upon the nature of human interaction to carry their message. While one does not have to win acting awards for one's reading, it is important to have some sense of how the human interaction affects the story and its participants. One must communicate the import of the story by a use of voice that differentiates among the characters and that carries some of their emotion. For example, read the story in 2 Samuel 18:1-19:8. One can sympathize with King David in his anguish over the death of his son. Yet one can feel the underlying anger of Joab, who had risked his life and those of his troops in battle to save a kingdom, whose monarch seemed scarcely to care. It is a moment of poignancy, one that has challenged musicians for centuries. Several have set it to song, with moving results. The story must communicate in its own terms. Being caught up in the lives of the people involved in the narrative is critical to communication. The reality of the actors in the narrative's drama, regardless of how strange the surroundings appear to us, is the key to communicating the Word of God in narrative reading.

Each literary style has its own means of communication

and one who reads is responsible that God's Word be communicated clearly. Since communication involves speaker and hearer at all times, but especially until one is used to the discipline of reading aloud, as well as to the particular place in which that reading is to be done, it is best to have someone monitor practice sessions and make suggestions. This is also helpful from time to time after one has become an "old pro" at the practice.

If one has problems, the local high school speech teacher or drama coach will probably be glad to help. The matter is central to one's responsibilities as a lay reader or lector. The accuracy and propriety with which the reading is done is an essential matter.

Saint Luke tells us that Jesus, on returning home to Nazareth, stood up in the synagogue to read. When one reads in the synaxis of the eucharist or in the Office, one follows Jesus' example and shares in that part of our Lord's ministry. It is a privilege which one should treasure and prepare for carefully.

LAY PARTICIPATION
IN THE EUCHARIST

In addition to reading lessons, there are several other things in the eucharist that can be done by lay persons.

The Prayers of the People

In the directions included in Concerning the Celebration on pp. 322 and 354 of the BCP it is said that ". . . Lay persons . . . may lead the Prayers of the People." This is reinforced on p. 328, where the rubric states that *the Deacon or other person appointed says* Let us pray for the whole state of Christ's Church and the world." The clear implication is that the priest does not lead the Prayers of the People. The same is true in the rubrics introducing each of the six forms of intercession for Rite II of the eucharist on pp. 383-393 of the BCP. In the case of the Rite II Prayers of the People, the celebrant concludes the prayers with an appropriate collect and may introduce them with a sentence of invitation.

Of greater significance as far as the leader of the prayers is concerned is the rubric on p. 383 that allows that "adaptations or insertions suitable to the occasion may be made." Needless to say, these are to be done at the discretion of and under the direction of the celebrant, but it does provide opportunity to have specific prayers for persons or concerns within the congregation. This is achieved in Forms I and V by the use of blanks in some of the petitions and the blank petitions. Forms II, III, IV, and VI include specific places for individuals within the congregation to add their specific concerns.

In some congregations, special intercession lists are kept and used at liturgy. If that is the case, the lay leader needs to be sure that the list has been preread and that any unusual names have been mastered. It may be necessary to find a way of adapting the language of the prayers so that the names or concerns fit flowingly into the Prayer Book texts.

Whether or not there are parish lists, it is important that ample opportunity be given for members of the congregation to include their concerns in Prayers of the People. It is hard to suggest how much time should be left in each period marked *silence* or where silence is implied. It is similarly hard to recommend surefire ways of assuring that a congregation will begin becoming active participants in the Prayers of the People. The title itself clearly implies congregational participation. If not, they could well be labeled "Prayers for the People." In cooperation with the celebrant, however, the lay leader of the intercessions needs to find ways to encourage participation.

The Offertory

While not specifically the responsibility of those who take part in the leadership of the service, nonetheless, the role of the laity in the Offertory cannot be overlooked, if one is to do justice to lay involvement in the eucharist. The rubric on pp. 333 and 361 makes it clear that the presentation of the bread and wine is to be done by lay representatives. The bread and wine are to be presented in the same way and at the same time as the money and other gifts.

The bread and the wine represent the life of the congregation. They are a particularly apt representation, since each is the product of a God-given gift (wheat or grapes) and our use of the gift. Each is the product of the whole social order and economy of which we are part. Farmers, processors, trans- porters, salespersons, retailers, and the tax collector all are involved in the creation of bread from wheat and wine from grapes. Each is the product of the diversity and complexity of our culture. Each is, as well, something that can do great good or great ill—like all of life. While it is "wine that maketh glad the heart of man," it is also the misuse of wine that has destroyed many lives and broken many families. While bread is the "staff of life," many overeat and diet while a larger part of the world starves. The best and worst of all of us is included in the bread and wine we bring to present so that they may become the body and blood of Christ.

The rubric is clear that it is "representatives of the congregation" who bring the oblations of bread and wine, who offer the life of the congregation to God. (Please note that the rubrics suggest that at baptism the newly baptized or the godparents present the oblations; that at confirmation, the confirmands do so; and that at a marriage, the newly married present the oblations.) In considering lay participants in worship, the priest and lay leadership should take serious note of the importance of this lay involvement. The persons need to be chosen with care, in order to underline the privilege it is to present the oblations.

Lay Eucharistic Ministers

Title III, Canon 3, provides two other ways in which a lay person can be involved in the Eucharist: as a licensed chalice bearer; and as one licensed by the bishop and commissioned by the priest, to take the Sacrament to the shut-ins immediately upon the conclusion of the liturgy. Customs vary widely as regards acceptance of these practices, as well as requirements for training and license. If anyone is interested in pursuing either ministry, it will be necessary to consult with the parish priest in one's congregation to discover whether either of these ministries is authorized in that particular parish and, if so, what the requirements are for licensure.

LAY PARTICIPATION
IN THE OFFICE

The Nature and Structure of the Office

Although the lay minister works under the direction of a priest or bishop, from time to time it will be necessary to plan and officiate at Morning or Evening Prayer when it is a principal service of Sunday worship. It is possible to do so simply by following the rubrics, but it is easier if one has some notion of the rationale and structure of the Office.

There are three prime determinants of any service of Morning or Evening Prayer. First, and most generally, there is the rationale for the service, as the BCP defines it. Second, and somewhat more specifically, there is the season of the Christian year in which the service is being offered. Third, and most specifically, the lessons for the day provide the Office's most immediate context.

Taking first things first, in a passage derived from all the prayer books since 1552, the 1979 *Book of Common Prayer* defines the purpose of the Office thus: ". . . we have come together in the presence of Almighty God our heavenly Father, . . . to set forth his most worthy praise, to hear his holy Word, and to ask, for ourselves and on behalf of others, those things that are necessary to our life and salvation. . . ." (BCP, pp. 41 and 79). When we hear the Word of God in the Office, we respond with praise for God's majesty and with prayer for our weakness. In such a pattern, the proclamation of the Word of God is central, and the response from the faithful is related to that proclamation. If we view the Office in a pattern of proclamation and response, the structure looks like this:

Introduction to the Office
The Liturgy of Praise
　The invitatory and psalter as proclamation
　The *Gloria patri* as a response of praise
The Liturgy of the Word
　The lessons as proclamation
　The canticles as response
　The sermon or homily as proclamation (*N.B.* This may appear
　　elsewhere)
The creed as summary response to the liturgy of the Word
The Liturgy of Prayer
　The prayers are the response of the People of God to the Word
　　of God
Conclusion of the Office

In this outline, the pattern of proclamation and response is quite clear, and provides a rational structure within which to make the various choices that must be made by the officiant.

Planning of the Office

Any time one plans any service, there is a series of decisions that must be made, particularly if the service is to have an internal coherence. In order to rationalize and simplify these decisions, the following worksheet has been prepared. In the text of this book, the decisions themselves will be discussed. The worksheet will provide a listing of the alternatives and a place to record the choices.

The first prerequisite to planning any service is a Church calendar. Most parishes have one. Morehouse Publishing sells a calendar that includes the lesson choices and some hymn choices. Since the lessons for the eucharist and the Office are ordinarily the same (*cf.*, the rubric in the second paragraph of BCP. p. 888), it will be particularly useful. On pp. 19-30 of the BCP, there is a month-by-month listing of all the commemorations. Be sure to check it, and list any commemoration for the day. If there is not going to be a eucharist on any major holy day of the week (printed in boldface type), you may wish to include the commemoration in the Office. This calendar information provides the "spine" from which the rest of the choices about the Office depend.

Having found the calendar information one must decide whether to use Rite I or Rite II. Both Morning and Evening Prayer come in two styles: traditional or contemporary. Rite I is in the traditional "thee/thou" and "-eth/-est" forms. Rite II uses the vernacular "you" for the second person and verbs in their customary form. In addition to the difference in language, the Morning Prayer version of Rite II has a number of additional canticles to be used after the lessons. Where Rite I provides seven, Rite II provides fourteen. Aside from these differences, however, the two are identical. The Rite II canticles may be used with Rite I (BCP, p. 47). The Morning Prayer canticles may be used with Evening Prayer (BCP, p. 65).

When a choice of form has been made, set about selecting among the options that make up the Office. A careful reading of the rubrics will show that in the BCP great emphasis is given to the seasons of the Church year. This book, with the books since 1892, provides seasonal opening sentences. In addition, there are seasonal canticles and invitatories. Since there are a large number of canticles, those responses can be specifically targeted to the lessons for which they are a response. Since the opening sentences and the antiphon or invitatory set the whole tone of the service, it is well to look at them carefully and give considerable thought to their implications.

There are several ways to open the Office. One must use the versicle, "Lord, open our lips," (BCP, p. 80 or p. 42) in Morning Prayer or its equivalent, "O God, make speed to save us" (BCP, p. 117 or p. 63) in Evening Prayer. In addition, one may preface that versicle with an opening sentence, general or proper to the season. If one wishes to do so, after the sentence one may use a general confession introduced by either a long or a short invitation. Please note that the proper form for the absolution to be used by a lay reader is in the rubric immediately following the priestly absolution. When these decisions have been made, note them on the worksheet. Note that the "alleluia" is *not* used during Lent.

The Invitatory follows the Preces. At Evening Prayer, there is only one printed, but those for Morning Prayer may be read. At Morning Prayer, one must choose among three options. The *Venite* is the one that was provided in the prayer books beginning in 1549. The *Jubilate* has followed the second lesson as an optional canticle since 1552. It now has been moved to a position as an alternative Invitatory. Seasonal and general antiphons have been provided for these two invitatories (BCP, p. 43 and 81). The third option has even a more complex history. The bulk of *Pascha nostrum* was arranged from texts of St. Paul by Archbishop Cranmer as a paschal introit. It was used thus in the 1549 book. In 1552 it was used as an Easter Sunday substitute for the *Venite*. In 1662, the opening section (I Cor. 5:7-8), not included earlier, was added and the *Gloria patri* was attached at the end. Now *Pascha nostrum* joins the rest of the invitatories and may be used throughout the paschal season until the day of Pentecost. One of the three must be used. Place is given on the worksheet for that choice.

The psalm is found in the lectionary for the Sunday. If your calendar does not list the lessons, then determine the cycle year and the Sunday within it and look in the lectionary. This starts on p. 889 with the First Sunday in Advent for Year A. It lists all the possible Sundays for Year A. It then lists Year B and Year C the same way. Following Year C, on p. 921, the lessons for the Holy Days that appear in the calendar in bold face print are listed. The readings following Holy Days are not for Sunday use. The rubric notes that if the selected psalm has a longer

ORDER FOR THE DAILY OFFICE

	Hymnal	Prayer Book
The opening hymn	_____	
The opening sentences: yes/no		_____
The Confession and absolution: yes/no		

	Hymnal	Prayer Book
The preces	_____	_____
The Invitatory	_____	_____
The psalm(s)		_____
The first reading		
The canticle	_____	_____
The second reading		
The canticle	_____	_____
The third reading (optional)		
The sermon (optional at this point)		
The creed		_____
The Lord's Prayer		_____
The Suffrages: A/B	_____	_____
The Collect for the day		_____
The Office collects		_____

| The Office hymn or anthem (optional) | _____ | |

The sermon (optional at this point)		
The prayers: #s _____ or		
The Great Litany		_____
Other devotions		_____
The grace		_____

| The sermon (optional here or after collection) | | |
| The collection, with hymn or anthem | _____ | |

| The closing devotions | | _____ |
| The closing hymn | _____ | |

N.B. Everything within the box must be included in the Office, unless it is marked "optional." Everything with a single bar on the left side is either optional or flexible.

and a shorter number of verses listed, the longer selection is to be used for Morning or Evening Prayer. The psalm always ends with the *Gloria patri.*

After the recitation of the psalm, the lessons are read with canticles after the first two readings. One must, therefore, determine how many readings there are to be and which ones to select. When the Office is the main service on a Sunday, it is inappropriate to have fewer than two readings. If one is to have two readings, the first must always be from the Old Testament (BCP, p. 934). For a second lesson, the choice is between the two readings from the New Testament, if one is going to have only two readings. Although there are no criteria for choice in the rubrics of the BCP, the following considerations are reasonable.

If the Sunday is in a green season, the choice should be made so that the Old Testament lesson will match the New Testament lesson. Since the Old Testament lesson ordinarily matches the Gospel lesson, the continuity of the course reading will be kept. If the Sunday is in a special season, since the readings are not in course, the criterion for choice is the extent to which the Old Testament lesson, and whatever New Testament reading is chosen, underline the season's theme. Remember that the Old Testament lessons in Lent have their own coherence.

Since the Office is historically the service of the Word, and since the lesson choices are deliberately laid out to provide a balanced knowledge of Scripture, one can maintain that there is value in using three lessons, rather than two. Although the rubrics make a three-lesson Office an option, and although two lessons have been the norm for the last century or so, for the first three centuries of our separate existence, Anglicans ordinarily heard full Morning Prayer and ante-communion on a Sunday morning. This provided four lessons. There is, therefore, a sense in which three lessons is an "Anglican compromise."

Whatever the decision on lessons, it is important to read them ahead, preferably aloud. Note the rubric on announcing the lessons. The announcement is: "A Reading (Lesson) from _____." One may also announce the chapter and verse. At the conclusion of the lection, one may simply say: "Here ends (or endeth) the Lesson (Reading)." One may, however, finish the lection by saying: "The Word of the Lord." To this, the congregation is to respond: "Thanks be to God." It is to be assumed that parish customs (under the direction of the rector) will grow up around this and will rapidly become the local norm.

When there are two readings, each reading is accompanied by a canticle. All of the canticles to be found in Rite I are to be found in Rite II. Rite II has seven additional canticles. Of the canticles available in Morning Prayer I, only the *Benedictus Dominus Deus* has any particular seasonal connotation. In the 1928 book, the *Benedictus* could be shortened except in Advent, vaguely implying that *Benedictus* (in its full form) was an Advent canticle. There is a negative connotation, however, in the tradition that neither the *Te Deum laudamus* nor the *Gloria in excelsis* is used during Advent or Lent. The rules governing the use of the *Gloria in excelsis* in the Eucharist are found on p. 406 of the BCP. In the Office there is no provision that the *Gloria* must be used, but the rule as to when it should not be used can be considered to apply. The custom concerning the *Gloria* is parallel to the one concerning the *Te Deum*. Beyond these customs, there is no particular guide to the use of canticles in Morning Prayer I.

Morning Prayer II, in addition to providing twice as many options as Morning Prayer I, provides one canticle, *The Song of Moses* or *Cantemus Domino* (#8), which is particularly suitable for Easter. It provides another, *A Song of Penitence* or *Kyrie Pantokrator* (#14), that is especially suitable for Lent. In addition to these, and in addition to the canticles available in both Morning Prayer I and II, as described above, several of the more general canticles have reminiscences of other seasons. *Quaerite Dominum* (#10) is rather more penitential than some of the others. *Surge, illuminare* (#11) quotes some of the customary Epiphany lections. It and *Ecce, Deus* (#9) would both appear particularly suitable for Advent and Epiphany. Remember, Advent is concerned with the second epiphany of Christ as judge; Epiphany is concerned with the manifestation of the power of God in the first epiphany of Jesus. It is, therefore, not surprising that some of the liturgical material is interchangeable. (*Cf.*, Hymn 640, used in both seasons, as is Hymn 76.) *If a third lesson is read, no canticle follows it.*

The purpose of the canticles is to provide a vehicle for the response of the faithful to the proclamation of the Word of God. In special seasons, the seasonal thrust is important to the response. In green seasons, however, it will be important to match the canticle as closely as possible to the general tenor of the lesson that preceded it. Since the readings are in course, there will be many themes struck throughout both the longer and the shorter green season. For the Office to have integrity, it is important to choose the canticles with particular care. Appropriate musical settings of all the invitatories and canticles are to be found in the front of *The Hymnal 1982* (Nos. S 1-66, S 177-288).

As we noted above, unless especially licensed by the bishop, a lay reader may not preach. Responsibility for the arrangements to be made for the explication of the Word rests ultimately on the lay reader and the ecclesiastical authority under whom the lay reading is done. Although it is not the provenance of a general handbook to discuss how the preaching is arranged, it is important to remember that preaching the Word is a vital part of its proclamation. Arrangement should be made, therefore, for a homily or sermon of some kind.

The rubrics permit the sermon to occur in one of three places: after the lessons, in conjunction with the office hymn after the third collect, or after the Office. When the Office has been the main service the sermon has traditionally been preached after the Office, either before or after the collection of the alms. The service has then ended with additional prayers and a dismissal in some form. The continuation of that pattern is implied by the rubrics on pp. 141ff. of the BCP.

The following diagram outlines the structural relationship between the Office and that portion of the eucharist that precedes the Offertory (which is known technically, from its Greek name, as the *Proanaphora*). This relationship provides the logic for preaching after the lessons, which is the place required by the rubric in the eucharist. The service then would end with an offering, closing prayers, and dismissal. There is a certain inherent logic in associating the preaching of the Word with the proclamation of the Word.

Although it does not spell it out exactly, the third alternative would provide the most coherent structure of the three options. Under the options provided by the rubrics, after the third collect there would be a hymn or anthem. When it was finished, there would be a sermon. Since the rubric permits an offering "at the Office," presumably it could be taken following the sermon, and then the closing prayers of the Office and the grace would finish the service. The disjunction that comes from two sets of prayers and two conclusions, a grace, and a dismissal would be avoided.

The same simplification could be accomplished if the sermon were preached after the lessons by taking up the offering during the office hymn or anthem and using the period of prayer and thanksgiving with the grace as the conclusion of the Office.

There are advantages to all three options. There are limitations to each. But, since the shape of the Office will be affected by the decision, it must be made at this point in the planning process.

Patterns of Worship
Ministry of the Word and Morning Prayer

Holy Communion	Morning Prayer
Acclamation	
	Opening sentences
Penitential Order	Confession
Collect for Purity	
Summary of the Law	
	Preces
Kyrie, Gloria, or Trisagion	Invitatory
Salutation and Collect	
	Psalm
Lesson I	**Lesson I**
Psalm, hymn, or anthem	**Canticle**
Lesson II	**Lesson II**
Psalm, hymn, or anthem	**Canticle**
Lesson III (Gospel)	Lesson III
Sermon	Sermon
Creed	**Creed**
Prayers of the People	**Lord's Prayer**
	Suffrages and Collects
Confession	
	Office hymn
	Prayers
Peace	**Grace**

Items in bold print are those that must be used. Those in plain print are those that are optional.

The Apostles' Creed is the overall response of the faithful to the proclamation of the Word of God. It is always used when the Office is the main Sunday service. The text of the Apostles' Creed is in the ICET translation in Rite II.

When it became clear that many communions within the Church were beginning to use liturgical forms and that many others, throughout the world, were either translating or revising their established liturgies, the time appeared propitious to produce a translation of the liturgical texts that could be used in common by all Christians who worship in English. To produce such texts an international interfaith committee called the International Consultation on English Texts (ICET) was founded. The ICET retranslated all of the common texts used in the Eucharist and in the Office, including the Nicene and Apostles' Creeds.

In the BCP, the ICET texts are used in Rite II, the traditional texts in Rite I, and the ICET Lord's Prayer is set side by side with the traditional translation in Rite II.

The ICET's only significant departure from the customary text paraphrases the rubrical suggestion in all the American Books of Common Prayer, which said: "And any Churches may, instead of the words, *He descended into hell*, use the words, *He went into the place of departed spirits*, which are considered as words of the same meaning in the Creed" (1928 BCP, pp. 15 and 29). Hence, "He descended to the dead" (*cf.*, I Peter 3:19).

The Collects and the Prayers

Within the Office we have a recurring pattern of proclamation and response. The canticles act as the immediate response of the faithful to the proclamation. The creed is the overall response to the proclamation. The service of prayer is the result of the proclamation. Having heard and having responded, we are impelled, by the nature of the Word, to _do_ something. The best and first thing that we do is pray.

Since the Office provides considerable flexibility in choice of both collects and prayers, it is appropriate to establish some criteria for choice.

First, since the Office is a corporate activity of praise and worship, it is important that the prayers reflect the life and needs of the faithful. Hence, "In the Intercessions and Thanksgivings, opportunity may be given for the members of the congregation to express intentions or objects of prayer and thanksgiving, either at the bidding, or in the course of the prayers; and opportunity may be given for silent prayer" (BCP, p. 142). Certainly, if no opportunity is given for personal intercession, there is some responsibility on the part of the officiant for the maintenance and use of an intercession and thanksgiving list.

Second, the prayer life of the congregation should be balanced. It should serve as a reminder of those needs in our lives and the lives of others to which our sin blinds us. This is one of the ways to keep prayer from being a monologue from ourselves to God. To this end, the BCP lists those things that should be included in a full balanced life of intercession. The list is found on p. 383 of the BCP.

There are three ways in which this balance can be achieved. To take them in the order in which they occur in the BCP, there is the Great Litany that begins on p. 148 (see Hymnal S 67); there are the Prayers of the People that begin on p. 383; there are Prayers and Thanksgivings that begin on p. 810. These will be discussed in greater detail later.

The service of prayer begins with the salutation and Lord's Prayer, unless the Great Litany is to be used, in which case the Lord's Prayer may be omitted. If Rite II is to be used, the version of the Lord's Prayer to be used must be determined and should be noted.

There are two sets of suffrages, the earlier a variation of the traditional suffrages. In Morning Prayer the second set of suffrages derives from the third section of the *Te Deum*. This is a wandering liturgical text that at one point was appended to the *Gloria in excelsis* and then to the *Te Deum*. It is a good text that fits neither of its former hosts and now finds a home, quite appropriately, as the Suffrages at the Morning Office. The second evening set is in litany form with a fixed response. A choice must be made between the sets of suffrages, and note made of that choice.

The collects reflect something that is at times forgotten: the Office is a daily offering of Word, prayer, and praise. The clergy are expected to read the daily Office. The laity would benefit if they did. There are specific collects for three days of the week, which stand as reminders of the daily nature of the recitation of the Office. They also are a weekly reminder of the death, burial, and resurrection of our Lord.

The rubric on use of the collects simply requires that one or more be used. The traditional number of collects is three. Whatever number of collects one determines to use, the collect of the day should be used. This can be found in traditional or contemporary form on the pages following p. 159.

Whatever number and selection one makes from the five other available collects, that selection should, as far as is possible, reflect the general tenor of the season and the lections. One of the three "prayers for mission" will rarely be used, as they are only to be used if no other general intercession is offered, which would be unacceptable at the main service on a Sunday. They, or the collects on p. 394f. can be used, however, as the summary collects to the various Prayers of the People.

Before one chooses the prayers to be used after the collects one has chosen, it is important not only to be aware of the categories that should be covered but to be thoroughly familiar with all of the options. If the officiant reads the Office daily, that will probably guarantee familiarity. A lay reader should probably submit to the necessary spiritual discipline of a daily routine of prayer and Bible reading. If, however, the officiant does not read the Office daily, it will be necessary to read through the various alternatives and become thoroughly familiar with them.

The first alternative is the Great Litany. This prayer, which is all-inclusive, was the first piece of the Prayer Book to be published in English. It dates from 1544, five years before the first Book of Common Prayer. It has, of course, been updated and edited over the years, but it remains one of the first examples of liturgical prayer in the English language. Note that there is a special devotion (also derived from the 1544 Litany) for use in times of war, anxiety, or disaster. This Supplication is found on p. 154 and can be used either at the end of the Litany, or after the third collect, or separately. In an uncertain and anxious world, the Supplication should be part of our repertory of prayer.

The second set of alternatives is the series of six intercessions from the eucharist. There is considerable flexibility in both form and language. Form I, derived from the traditional Eastern Rite litany, is formal and allows minimum opportunity for special intercessions. Form II, in contrast, is simply a series of biddings, with silence in between, into which either concerned individuals in the congregation, or the officiant on behalf of the congregation can intersperse the special intercessions of the faithful. Form III is a set of extended versicles and responses, with opportunity for the faithful to add special intercession at the end. Form IV consists of a series of biddings, with silence, followed by a fixed versicle and response. There is no rubrical mention of special intercessions. Form V is a litany, similar in form and content to Form I, with more flexibility for particular intercessions. Form VI is also in the versicle-response form but with increased opportunity for congregational participation. It also has an optional form for general confession appended. Forms I-IV require a summary collect. Form V has an alternative doxology. Form VI permits either an absolution or a collect. Since an absolution requires a priest, a collect would be used by a lay reader. Appropriate collects follow the Prayers of the People. None of these includes a thanksgiving, which should be used in addition, if Prayers of the People are used.

The BCP provides many pages of prayers and thanksgivings, which include general prayers as well as a number of more specific intercessions. There is a complete table of contents on pp. 810-813 with appropriate cross references. It is important to know these pages of prayers intimately, since they provide the largest resource for both the prayers after the third collect and the prayers after the offering.

Probably more than in any of the preceding Prayer Books, this collection of Prayers and Thanksgivings provides material for specific thanksgivings. The range of topics is far larger and provides the opportunity for specific thanksgivings, followed by the General Thanksgiving as a kind of summary.

The collect for Proper 28 urges us to "read, mark, learn, and inwardly digest" the Scriptures. The same suggestion should be made for the Prayers and Thanksgiving section of the BCP.

Whatever course one chooses for the service after the third collect, it should be remembered that a hymn or anthem is permitted, and probably should be used, after the third collect and before whatever follows. (*Cf.*, above for alternate endings to the Office.)

Whatever decision is made, provision is made for it on the worksheet. Determine what is to be done, and then make careful note, so that during the Office there will be no hitch, no unseemly delay, no rustling of papers.

By now all the basic decisions regarding the Office have

been made. Hymns are still to be chosen. Closing prayers, if any, have to be put into place. But, the essential work is done.

To review: the rite has been chosen; the type of beginning, general or penitential, has been determined; the number and choice of lessons and canticles is settled; the position of the sermon is established; the choice of suffrages and the selection of collects has been noted; the prayers after the third collect are selected and listed.

When all this is accomplished, read through the service aloud and in the place where you will officiate. Make sure that everything fits together, that the theme of the Sunday and season is prominent. Be sure that the concerns of the faithful are included in the prayers. Mark the psalm, the collect for the day and the prayers after the third collect, so that there will be no fumbling. When all has been done that can be done to select carefully, when one has prepared thoughtfully and prayerfully, then God the Holy Spirit will see that everything is done "decently and in order."

The Ministry of the Word as a
Sunday Alternative

One of the hallmarks of the BCP is its emphasis on the centrality of the eucharist. The initial rubric in the BCP refers to the eucharist as ". . . the principal act of Christian worship on the Lord's Day. . . ." The Pastoral Offices use, as their shape, the ministry of the Word from the eucharistic rites. As the eucharist becomes the principal act of worship throughout the Church, the Office may become a fairly unknown liturgy. Should this become the case, when a lay reader is required to take services in the absence of a priest, there may be a problem of congregational recognition of and participation in the Office. In that case, the BCP provides a remedy.

The bottom rubric on p. 406 provides an order of service when there is to be no communion. It consists of the ministry of the Word, the Prayers of the People, music for gathering of the offerings of the people, and a close to the service. Provision is made at the beginning of the rite for a penitential preparation. For many congregations, this would be liturgy in which they could participate more fully and more comfortably. Its outline would (or could) look like this:

Opening hymn
Penitential Order, Rite I or II (optional) or
Opening of Rite I or II
Kyrie/Trisagion/*Gloria in excelsis*
Salutation and Collect
Lesson(s)
Psalm, hymn or anthem (optional)
Gospel
Sermon
Creed
Announcements (optional)
Prayers of the People
Ingathering of alms and its accompanying music
Lord's Prayer
Grace/Peace
Closing hymn

It is important to read rubrics 2-10 of Additional Directions on pp. 406ff., since they provide at least some of the options available to the celebrant. Since these options are new, it is advisable to review them briefly, step by step.

First, the service should never be read from the altar. It is a ministry of the Word. The rubric suggests that the lessons be read from pulpit or lectern. The whole thrust of the BCP is to return the liturgy, as much as possible, to the people. Certainly the Word should be proclaimed in their midst. The liturgy should be celebrated from some point in proximity to the faithful. The place should, if possible, underline the connection between the rest of the rite and the proclamation of the Word.

If a penitential liturgy is desired, it must come at the outset of the service by use of the Penitential Order. This order is printed directly before each form of the eucharistic rite. After the opening versicle/response the Decalogue is permitted. The Summary of the Law is available but is only one of three scriptural verses that may be used. After the confession, the lay reader remains kneeling to read the statement of forgiveness, using "us" rather than "you."

If the celebrant determines not to use the Penitential Order, the ministry of the Word is begun in accordance with its own rubrics (p. 323 or p. 355).

The first choice that one must make is among the Kyrie, Trisagion, or Gloria. The rubrics on p. 406 indicate when the Gloria must, may, or may not be used. In making the decision, refer first to that rubric. The Gloria must be used during festal seasons. It may not be used during preparatory seasons. It is optional during green seasons. If the Gloria may not be used, then the choice between the other two is determined largely on subjective factors. If the Gloria *may* be used, then the decision whether or not to do so, while subjective, should include such factors as the general tone of the lessons and the other music in use for that Sunday. Note that in Rite I the Gloria *and* Kyrie or Trisagion may be used. In Rite II, however, the Gloria *or* Kyrie *or* Trisagion is used. The method for use of Kyrie or Trisagion is discussed in the rubric on p. 406.

When it comes to lesson choices, everything that has been said previously about the Office applies to the ministry of the Word. Here, as in the Office, there is no psalm, hymn, or anthem following the Gospel. It is to be assumed that "hymn" in the rubric following the description of the lessons (which reads, "A Psalm, hymn, or anthem may follow each reading") includes the canticles from the Office. The rubrics covering the matter of music are on p. 14.

The Nicene Creed in Rite I is printed in the ICET text as well as the older translation. In Rite II only the ICET text is available.

Where possible, the choice between these two should be based upon parish custom. The ICET texts have been discussed earlier.

If announcements have not been made before the service or will not be made at its conclusion, they should be made after the creed. They should, under no circumstances, interfere with the flow of the rite.

If one is using Rite I, the Prayer for Christ's Church and the World may be used, with or without an "appropriate response" after each paragraph. In addition, any of the six intercessions available for Rite II may be used. When using Rite II, only the forms following p. 385 are appropriate. Note that the rubric on p. 814 limits the use of the Prayers and Thanksgiving section following that page to "after the Collects of Morning or Evening Prayer, or separately." It would, therefore, be improper to use prayers from this section with the ministry of the Word.

The service concludes simply enough with the gathering of the alms of the congregation, the recitation of the Lord's Prayer and either the grace or the exchange of the Peace. The rubric on p. 407 explains the exchange of the Peace.

The service may, of course, begin and end with music.

The Minor and Pastoral Offices

This section of the book will deal exclusively with those portions of the BCP that have a role for the laity other than as officiant at the Office or lector. For simplicity's sake, the discussion will follow the order of the rites as they are printed in the BCP.

The Order for Noonday is quite straightforward and requires nothing more than to read the rubrics carefully and follow them exactly. An Order of Worship for the Evening is a little more complicated but indeed may prove useful for devotions when no priest is available to celebrate the eucharist. Like the Office, this order is particularly appropriate for a lay reader, since it is a service of the Word. When reading through the rite, the first thing to note is the existence of "short lessons" for the seasons on p. 108 and special collects for the seasons on p. 111. The service can be used for many occasions, but it cannot stand alone. It is assumed that there will be some form of completing rite: the Office, the eucharist, or the less structured form provided on p. 113. Whatever follows this rite, however, should also carry the seasonal or occasional significance provided by its lessons and hymns.

Because of the possible seasonal impact of this rite, as it is prepared, it might be advisable to refer to the section of this study that outlines the nature and meaning of the seasons in the Church calendar. Note that this rite is *not* appropriate during Holy Week, except for Maundy Thursday. It is primarily a festal introduction to evensong or some other evening service or activity. Note that a lay minister may officiate when a bishop or priest is present. Be aware of the rubrics surrounding that circumstance. They are found on p. 108.

Since the purpose of this rite is to create a special ambience for worship, it is important to follow the directions on pp. 142f. with great care. They outline the use of the candle, the lighting of lights, and the possible use of incense to underline the particular tone of this rite. Read them with care and be sure that any supporting persons, such as organist, choir, and servers, are carefully rehearsed. What one does easily in the light becomes exceedingly difficult in the dark.

The Order for Compline is straightforward. It is a lay office. No changes or substitutions are necessary.

The lay minister may officiate at all of the proper liturgies for special days except Maundy Thursday. This permission is granted, however, only in the absence of a member of the ordained ministry. These liturgies are those for the special days of Lent: Ash Wednesday, Palm Sunday, Good Friday, and

Easter Eve. They are of particular importance for a lay reader in charge of a congregation.

The Ash Wednesday liturgy is self-sufficient. It contains all the elements necessary for an Office. The directions are complete and self-explanatory. Note particularly that the lay minister substitutes the prayer for forgiveness from Morning Prayer for the absolution, and *remains kneeling.*

The service includes a prayer before the imposition of ashes. It may be used and ashes imposed, if that is the parish custom. The lay minister may use the prayer over the ashes, since the prayer is used to set apart (not bless) the ashes. It is inappropriate, however, for a lay minister to make the sign of the cross over the ashes, as a priest would do. If ashes are imposed, they are made from palms from the previous Palm Sunday and usually imposed in the sign of the cross.

It would be appropriate, if there is more than one lay minister in the parish, or if the parish has other available lectors, that the reading of the lessons be shared among several persons.

The rite for Palm Sunday is not complete in itself, since it is a preface to the ministry of the Word. For a lay minister responsible for services, therefore, this rite should act as a preface, not to Morning Prayer, but to the ministry of the Word. The latter was discussed at some length earlier in this chapter.

As one did not make the sign of the cross over the ashes on Ash Wednesday, so one does not make it over the palms on Palm Sunday.

Several matters need to be attended to before the rite. Be sure that the palms are "stripped," that is, put into a large enough number of branches to be distributed easily to the members of the congregation.

As a matter of efficiency, it is of great importance that the movement required in the rite and its accompanying music be carefully worked out with the organist in advance. Some

accompanying musical instrument may be necessary if the
distribution of the palms and the reading of the lesson are to
take place elsewhere than in the church proper. The rubric
suggests that the first part of this rite not be held in the church,
and that the church be entered in a singing procession. If this
is to be done (and it is a good suggestion), then some pitch-
setting instrument must accompany the procession until such
time as the organ can be heard. (*N.B.* If a trumpeter from the
school band is available, there are several trumpet descants to
"All glory, laud, and honor" which the trumpeter could play
after leading the faithful into the Church in procession.)
Appropriate music is provided in The *Hymnal 1982*, numbers
153-157. The ministry of the Word relates to the passion story.
"Palm" Sunday music is inappropriate once the ministry of the
Word has begun. Whatever arrangements are made, plan them
with the organist well in advance.

    In the rite for Good Friday, the rubric again permits the
service, which can be self-contained, to be led by a lay minister
in the absence of a priest or deacon. The altar is ordinarily left
bare on Good Friday. Because of the solemnity of the occasion,
the ceremony is kept simple.

    Since a sermon is required by the rite, some arrangement
needs to be made to see that the Word is proclaimed. Although
it is not required, the proposal on the bottom of p. 277,
that the celebrant read the collect and another person the
biddings, will provide useful variety and can be managed
by a lay minister and an associate. The devotions before
the cross, if they are to be done, require planning and careful
reading of the rubrics, since specific music is suggested.
As is true of Palm Sunday, it is necessary to work out the
musical arrangements with the organist well in advance.
Please note the final rubric, that no blessing or dismissal
is used. Since the rubric is specific that there is no "pro-
cessional" music and the service "concludes" with a printed

prayer, it is to be assumed that there is no "recessional" music.

The rubrics permit a lay minister responsible for services in a congregation to read most of the Easter Vigil service. If the lay minister is to do so, it will be necessary to arrange with other persons in the congregation to share in the readings, to prepare the music, and to see that lights are lighted at the appropriate time. In essence, the purpose of the rite is to move the Church from the mourning of Good Friday to the joy of the resurrection. To this end, a single flame is kindled. The paschal candle is lighted from that flame. There is a rubric which allows the members of the congregation to receive candles and light them from the paschal candle as it is brought to the front of the church. If one plans to do so, preparations and directions must be given in advance. Liturgical action in the dark has built-in difficulties.

The paschal candle is brought to the front and placed in its stand, and the hymn of praise, *Exsultet*, is said or sung. If it is to be sung and one's own musical skills are limited, find someone in the choir or congregation who can sing and let him or her do it. The musical setting is in *The Altar Book* with music supplement. Both are available from the Church Hymnal Corporation. The congregational responses are found in *The Hymnal 1982*, S 68-S 70.

The biblical presaging of the resurrection is then read. At least two of the lessons and their canticles must be read, one of which must be the Exodus story. Lectors should be used for these readings. Because baptism is so intimately connected with the resurrection, the baptismal vows of the faithful are renewed. Remember that St. Paul tells that we were buried with Christ in our baptism so that, through Christ's resurrection we might embark upon a new life. In baptism we share our Lord's death so that we may also, in baptism, share a similar resurrection like his (Romans 6:2-5, paraphrased). After we have reminded ourselves that we are participants in the resurrection through baptism, all the candles are lighted, and the liturgy of the Word begins. Since the rubric requires a homily, some arrangement must be made to provide for the proclamation of the Word. Because the service symbolizes the movement from darkness to light, it is important that as little light as possible be used. There needs to be enough to read responses, lections, and the like, but no more until, at the singing of the *Gloria in excelsis* (a cry of praise unsung since the Last Sunday after the Epiphany), all the candles in the church are kindled. In that way, it is clear that the resurrection is proclaimed and present. The musical setting for the Litany is found in *The Altar Book* with music supplement. The response is found in *The Hymnal 1982* S 75.

In the sacramental rites for the eucharist and for baptism, the only role that a lay minister can fulfill is that which is assigned by the celebrant, who must be a priest or bishop. In the baptismal office, the only possible role is to lead the litany. There are celebrants who prefer to have some member of the baptismal party fulfill that role. Should no one be willing or able so to do, or should the celebrant prefer to have a lay minister do so as representative of the faithful, then the lay minister may be asked to lead the intercessory litany.

The rubric at the beginning of the eucharist (BCP, p. 322) reads: "Lay persons appointed by the celebrant should *normally* be assigned the reading of the Lessons which precede the Gospel, and *may* lead the Prayers of the People" (emphasis added). It is to be noted that, although lay-read lessons are considered the norm, they are not automatically assigned. The discretion remains with the priest of the parish.

The prayer for Christ's Church and the world, on pp. 328-330, is read entirely by the person appointed, with no addition by the celebrant. The Prayers of the People, on pp. 383-393, however, always end with a collect by the celebrant.

In either case, the celebrant may introduce the Prayers of the People by sentences of intention.

If a lay reader has primary responsibility for a congregation, it is important to know what pastoral offices may be performed. We will, therefore, follow through the Pastoral Offices to determine the responsibilities and privileges of a lay reader.

Confirmation is preeminently the bishop's office. Any person responsible for a congregation merely acts as his ancillary. There is, however, nothing in the rubrics to preclude a licensed catechist who has prepared a class of confirmands from presenting them to the bishop. (*cf.*, Title III, Canon 3, Sec. 6)

Since the rite for A Form of Commitment to Christian Service takes place in the context of a eucharist, it is to be presumed that the celebrant will have full responsibility.

A marriage is a sacramental act that requires a priest (or "where it is permitted by civil law," a deacon). It is *never* performed by a lay person acting in an ecclesiastical role. The rubrics assume that the lessons and the intercessions will be read by lay persons. It is likely, however, that they will be read by members of the wedding party or of the families involved.

Should there be no priest in a parish, there is no rubrical reason why the service for A Thanksgiving for the Birth or Adoption of a Child cannot be used by a lay minister, as long as the optional closing blessing is not used. Read the rubrics with care, and visit and plan with the parents before the service. This rite can be an important part of the building of family feeling within a congregation.

The rubric (BCP, p. 453) says that a lay person may always use Part I of the Ministration to the Sick. Regular hospital calling by members of a congregation, as well as by priest or lay minister, is helpful and supportive. The above-noted part of the office for Ministration to the Sick provides a formal role for a lay reader. The prayers on pp. 458-460 can well be used by a visiting lay minister or by friends from the congregation.

It might be well for a lay minister in charge of a congregation to provide copies of the prayers on p. 461 to be used by the sick person during illness.

There are two rites provided for the Burial of the Dead. Rite One is in more traditional language. Rite Two is in contemporary language. In addition, the second order is the more flexible and may be seen as the more "pastoral" of the two. Before beginning to plan the use of either rite, reading the appropriate general directions preceding each is extremely important. Many of the older traditions, recently neglected, are preserved and (in some cases) required. A closed casket, for example, is required. The custom of the celebrant accompanying the body from the hearse and to the grave is suggested.

Because of the extremely personal nature of the service, it is important, if one is in charge of a congregation, to meet with the family and plan the service with some care. The following form may be helpful in planning. If there is to be music, it is important to confer with the organist.

A further note on music: the rubric on p. 507 of the BCP says that "the liturgy for the dead is an Easter liturgy. . . ." The music of the liturgy, then, needs to reflect that perception.

The BCP provides several opportunities for ministry that have not previously been available. Although there has long been a Litany for the Dying, it has been for use only at the moment of death. The Prayer Book now provides prayers for use at a funeral parlor (BCP, p. 465). The form for the Ministration at the Time of Death may, however, be substituted. Often in our modern urban situation the only opportunity for friends to offer corporate prayer for the departed is the evening before at the funeral parlor. Now there is an appropriate form.

Another addition which can be helpful is the form for the Reception of the Body, on p. 466 of the BCP. If, as the rubrics propose, a pall or a flag is to be placed over the casket as the

Planning a Funeral

Name: _____

Address: _____

City, State, Zip _____

Phone(s) _____

PRELIMINARY QUESTIONS:

Do you have a cemetery plot?   Y/N
Has it been blessed   Y/N

Name of preferred funeral director?
Have arrangements been made there?   Y/N

Do you have your: Cemetery deed?   Y/N

If not, where is it to be found?

Are the remains to be: Interred/Cremated?   I/C

If the latter, before or after the funeral?   B/A

Is there to be music?   Y/N
Have arrangements been made for it?   Y/N

Additional comments:

52 A Lay Minister's Guide

family is preparing to accompany the body into the church, this time will be a strain on the mourners. A quiet moment of prayer and preparation is important. This form provides that moment.

Whichever rite the celebrant and the family decide upon needs to be prepared with care. Note that the burial office's pattern is that of the eucharist before the Peace (the *proanaphora*). The following form may be used for planning the liturgy for either rite.

The rite opens, traditionally, with "anthems" from scripture. The final rubric on the preceding page gives the alternatives for walking, standing, and the like. In Rite I, appropriate psalms are written out for use with the various readings. It might be well to read all of the suggested lections before making a choice. Since the choice of psalms is related to the lesson, try to use one that is similar in theme to the previous reading. Any combination of readings is possible, as long as no two are from the same collection. One may read an Old Testament lesson and a Gospel, or an Old Testament lesson and a New Testament lesson, or a New Testament lesson and a Gospel, or only one selection chosen from either the Old Testament lessons, the New Testament lessons, or the Gospels.

Following the final lesson choice, a homily may be preached if the celebrant is licensed. The Apostles' Creed may be said. One or the other (at the least) is an appropriate response to the reading of the Word.

Because we are dealing with the burial when there is no eucharist, the Lord's Prayer follows after the response to the final lesson (if there is a response) or the final lesson itself.

The intercessions provide two options. One may read the prayers printed following the rubrics on p. 480, or one may substitute some selection of prayers from those on pp. 487-489. The former option is less flexible but has the advantage of being printed where it is easily found by those following the service

Funeral Liturgy

The Burial Office

(The indented material is for use in Rite II only)

	Hymnal	BCP

The opening anthem(s)
  The opening anthem(s) II
  The hymn or psalm

The Collect

The Old Testament lesson:
The psalm: or
The canticle:

The New Testament lesson:
The canticle: or
The hymn: or
The psalm

The Gospel
The homily
The Apostles' Creed

The Lord's Prayer
The Prayers of the People

The Commital

	Hymnal	BCP

The anthem
The commital prayer
The Lord's Prayer
The Additional Prayers (optional)
The versicles and dismissal

in their books. The latter provides greater flexibility so that the service can be more personalized, more tailored to the immediate need. The decision should be based upon a pastoral concern for the needs of the bereaved.

The Commendation is a new section of the rite. Its purpose is explained in its title. It is the part of the liturgy that deals most directly with the deceased. If it is to be used, be sure that there are people in the congregation who will make the response.

The "anthems" provided for use as the body is borne from the church are new but fill a need. They should be used unless there is a congregational hymn being sung.

The Committal has clear rubrics and should provide no problem. Be sure, however, that some prearrangement is made about who will cast earth upon the coffin during the sentence of committal. For obvious reasons, there is not room for upset or fumbling at that point.

Rite II is much like the first in general outline. There is an alternative opening in the form of a responsorial anthem. Following the opening section, permission is given to announce the purpose or intention of the rite. The same lections are offered, but the psalms are not printed out. The same rules regarding lessons apply, however. A literal reading of the rubric on p. 495 at the bottom allows anyone who has a demonstrable reason to do so to speak. Presumably, under this permission, the lay minister with or without license may speak.

The Apostles' Creed is printed out. The same possibilities for prayers exist. The printed prayer is quite personal and applicable primarily to an active member of the congregation.

For the rest, the services follow the same pattern and the same suggested rules. The Order for Burial (p. 506), while occasionally appropriate, should, where possible, be prepared in consultation with a neighboring priest or the bishop.

In summary, if a lay minister is required to do so, it is

possible to read the entire service. It is important to confer with the family, the organist, and the funeral director. Be sure that the last is aware of the rubrics regarding closed coffin and the custom of accompanying the coffin into and out of the church and out of the hearse at the cemetery.

These are the pastoral offices, and these are the things that a lay minister is permitted to do.

APPENDICES

APPENDIX I

Music in Worship

Music and liturgy have long been closely associated. St. Paul recommends that Christians give themselves to "psalms and hymns and spiritual songs," and many scholars believe that there are traces of hymnody throughout the epistles. We still sing the canticles that St. Luke presents in the first chapter of his gospel. The monastic offices, upon which daily Morning and Evening Prayer are based, are always sung. It is not surprising, then, that when there is a revision of *The Book of Common Prayer*, a revision of the hymnal soon follows.

In the American tradition, Prayer Book and hymnody have always been closely connected. The first Book of Common Prayer had metrical psalms and hymns bound with it. Until late in the nineteenth century that remained true. With the rapid development of Anglican hymnody and the custom of assigning particular tunes to particular hymns and printing the tunes out, however, we finally developed two books. *The Hymnal 1916* complemented the developments in the 1896 BCP, *The Hymnal 1940* was companion to the 1928 BCP, and now *The Hymnal 1982* has been designed to meet the musical needs of *The Book of Common Prayer* that was approved in 1979.

Even a cursory study of its contents shows how carefully *The Hymnal 1982* has been designed to serve its stated purpose. The first section of the book contains musical settings for all of the sections of both Daily Office and Eucharist that traditionally are sung, as well as settings for occasional use, such as Baptism, the Litany, the Easter Vigil, and the like. The first section of hymnody follows the order in the BCP for the Daily Office. The next major section follows the Church Year, season by season. Then there follows the Prayer Book order of liturgies from Baptism through Consecration of a Church. The General Hymns are listed by topic and are followed by three miscellaneous sections titled: The Christian Life; Rounds and Canons; National Songs. Every need that may occur in the course of worship life is met by *The Hymnal 1982*. Perhaps it might be well to review what can be sung in liturgy, and where hymnody is appropriate.

In the Daily Office, everything from the preces, ("Lord, open our lips/O God make speed to save us") through the Office hymn after the third collect can be sung, except the lessons. *The Hymnal 1982* contains settings for everything the congregation sings except the psalms. Settings of the psalms are available from the Church Hymnal Corporation in a variety of forms. They provide the *Gradual Psalms* for all three years, for use in the Eucharist on Sundays and Festivals. Two new settings of the 150 psalms are available: *The Anglican Chant Psalter* and *A New Metrical Psalter*, which one would ordinarily use at a main service of Morning Prayer. They are printed to be sung by choir and congregation, using a refrain. Unlimited copies of these psalms may be made. This is a single permission. **Ordinarily, copying music is prohibited, and Churches are subject to significant penalties if they do so.** It is a form of stealing, prohibited by law and proscribed by scripture. The collection of metrical settings allows the psalms to be used as contemporary-like hymns, rather than ancient Hebrew hymnody. Every parish receives several mailings in the course of a year listing available resources.

One important feature of the service music section of *The Hymnal 1982* is the directions for using the chants that appear in the accompaniment edition. Its explanations are clear and precise. Both the general rationale of chant and the specific directions for reading the symbols that make chanting possible are explained. It has been said by one of the editors of the book that he rereads the introduction several times in the year. **It is critical that anyone planning to chant the service read the introduction!!** The resources available in *The Hymnal 1982* include both plainchant and Anglican chant settings for the canticles and a variety of settings for the eucharist from a wide variety of historical periods and styles. For officiants, additional musical resources are available in the Altar Book edition of the Holy Eucharist, printed by Church Publishing Incorporated.

There are several good reasons for considering chanting the service. First, it adds to the beauty of worship. It gives an "elevated tone," which helps us sense worship as something special, as a particular gift reserved for an offering to God. It is probably the most traditional way of officiating at worship. There is both evidence for and a postulated reconstruction of chant in the temple at Jerusalem in our Lord's time, and ample circumstantial evidence that chant was the norm early in the Church's life. Music was provided for the *1549 Book of Common Prayer*, and chanting the Office is the traditional norm in England. On a more practical level, chant, which can be defined as sung speech, serves at least two useful purposes. Singing a syllable projects it further than saying a syllable, so that sung speech is easier to hear without amplification. Sung speech tends to keep the congregational response together better than spoken response, since the music provides a framework. As we have seen, the Office as it is usually used in parish churches consists of the traditional Office, with additions to the beginning and the end. By singing the Office proper, one can clarify the structure of the whole service, which benefits general comprehension.

Music in the eucharist has customarily been divided between

the "Common," or that which is sung at every service, and the "Proper," or that which is specific to a particular service. The Common includes: the acclamation; the Gloria, Kyrie or Trisagion; the Creed; the Sanctus and Benedictus; the memorial acclamation; the Lord's Prayer; the fraction anthem; the dismissal. There are obvious seasonal variants among these, of course, but on every Sunday each of them is used (except the memorial acclamation, if one is using Rite I), and the variations are not dependent upon the lessons. The Proper includes: the Introit, or entry music; the gradual psalm; the music between the second and third lessons; the music at the Offertory; the music at communion. These vary week by week and the choices ordinarily reflect the lessons.

The Hymnal 1982 provides resources for each. In the Service Music section, there are settings for each of the parts of The Common for both Rite I and Rite II. (Note that settings for the Gloria in excelsis are not with the eucharist settings, but in the canticles for the Daily Office.) Unlike The Hymnal 1940, where one was provided with four complete settings, each part of the Common has a variety of settings, allowing one to do a "mix and match" as seems appropriate.

To find music for the Proper, which in our tradition usually means finding appropriate hymns, The Hymnal 1982 and its supplements provide significant help. In addition to the seasonal listings (hymns 47-293), the General Hymns are listed by topic. Some provide obvious help, such as "The Holy Trinity." In other cases one needs to be aware that "Jesus Christ our Lord" contains many hymns of seasonal usefulness that also have a more general application.

The indices at the back of The Hymnal 1982 are also a source of assistance. The index of Authors, Translators, and Sources, for example, lists all of the paraphrases of passages of scripture, which can be useful, especially if one wants to use a psalm paraphrase.

Some other sources of assistance are easily available. Church Publishing Incorporated has provided a series of Hymn Book Studies. All of them are valuable in learning to make full use of the resources in *The Hymnal 1982*. *Hymnal Studies Five* by Marion J. Hatchett, however, has a Sunday-by-Sunday list of appropriate choices for both Office and Eucharist. It also contains choices for all special services of both *The Book of Common Prayer* and *The Book of Occasional Services*. The Diocese of Minnesota has, for years, published a guide for hymn choice. In addition, almost every diocese has a Music Commission, whose role is to be useful in promoting music in the Church. The commission will always be glad to help where it can. It probably is listed in the Diocesan Journal, or an inquiry at diocesan headquarters can put one in touch with the commission in any diocese.

Careful cooperation among clergy, lay assistants, and the parish musician is always basic. It is important to note that the ordained person in charge of the congregation is the final authority, according to canon law. Although that authority may be delegated, the ultimate accountability rests upon the person in charge. The appropriate canon and rubric are printed on the inside of the title page of *The Hymnal 1982*. The cooperation becomes critical when it is determined that it is time to learn to sing something that previously had been said or that some expansion of the congregation's repertory of hymns is necessary. Sensitivity and tact are needed, as well as giving a good reason for changing or adding to accustomed ways. *Hymnal Studies Six* by Raymond Glover gives background on text and tune for seventy-seven of the new hymns in *The Hymnal 1982*. It can be a valuable resource in this regard.

Another way to become acquainted with the riches of *The Hymnal 1982* is to compare the list of authors and the list of composers in the appropriate indices and find those who are remembered in the Calendar on pp. 19-30 of the BCP. There is considerable overlap, and discovering the relationship between hymnal and the BCP is a useful activity. In view of the vast array of riches available to Episcopalians in both *The Book of Common Prayer* and *The Hymnal 1982*, it would be a shame not to explore and use them fully.

APPENDIX II

Translations of the Bible

Over the years an increasing number of versions of the Bible have been authorized by General Convention for use in public worship. The present list, through 1997, includes:

The Authorized, or King James Version (1611)
The English Revision (1881) or American Revision (1901)
The Revised Standard Version (1952); the New Revised Standard Version (1990)
The Jerusalem Bible (1966); the New Jerusalem Bible (1987)
The New English Bible with Apocrypha (1970)
Good News Bible in Today's English Version (1976)
New American Version (1970)
The Revised Standard Version: an Ecumenical Edition generally known as the "RSV Common Bible" (1973)
The New International Version (1978)
The Revised English Bible (1989)

This information can always be found in Title II, Canon 2.

A glance at the list above shows a rapid increase in the number of authorized versions since about 1966. This increase is based on three things, as is the choice one makes among versions: a desire for an accurate text; a desire for precise meanings to words; a desire for words and phrases that carry immediate and continuing impact in our own time.

When the King James Version was prepared in 1611, there was one available text for the Bible. It was a fairly modern text, far removed from the writing of the biblical books. Over the years, archaeological discoveries, search of ancient libraries, and increased interest all produced, first a trickle, and finally a flood of old biblical manuscripts. These have been read patiently and compared with other manuscripts, grouped into families, dated (when possible) and used to create a "standard" text that compares as closely as possible to what was written originally. An elaborate system of notation has been developed for scholars, so that they may know and compare each variant reading. In many English versions, the more important variants are printed in the footnotes. This process of textual improvement is ongoing and will probably never really be finished. Barring a major breakthrough, however, it is relatively stabilized. It is this approximate stability that helps account for the proliferation of versions.

One often only knows the meaning of a word by the associations it conjures up or by the other words with which it is ordinarily joined in daily use. In addition, in pre-printing times, when written material was all hand produced and expensive, common speech was less apt to be written down, so only the "literary" was available to later generations. In 1611, there was very little available material to help the translators find the precise meaning of the words with which they were dealing. Classical Greek was related to New Testament Greek more or less as Shakespeare's language is related to ours. There is a relationship. With a glossary or a good ear, we comprehend most of it. But in a real sense, it is not our language. The translators of 1611, with all the good will in the world, had a classical dictionary, and a few pages of words that occur only in the New Testament. The task of producing an accurate translation was formidable. The result is astounding. In the years, particularly since the First World War, when fortunate finds in Egypt opened up new worlds of everyday vocabulary of first-century Greek and the discovery and translation of languages close to Hebrew pointed up the meaning of some obscure Hebrew vocabulary, things have moved very rapidly indeed. Unknown words have found precise meanings; odd phrases have been illumined. A more accurate text has been joined to more accurate translations of that text.

All of these translations attempt, in various idioms, to communicate the particularity of the biblical message from its ancient context to our modern one. Their authorization by the Church is a warrant of their suitability for liturgical use. The Jerusalem Bible and later versions will contain the textual and vocabulary knowledge and insights presently available. The choice among them, in the long run, depends upon how well the language of a particular version communicates to the individual lay reader and the congregation he or she is serving.

Most of these versions are available in inexpensive paperback. The parish library ought to have them anyway. Get a number of them. Use each for a few weeks, until ears have grown accustomed to the individual cadences. It is not essential that any one parish use only one translation. As preparation is made for a service, it would be well to read the lessons in several versions. It is likely that the version that one finds clearest will also be clearest to many in the congregation. The primary purpose of reading the Word is to communicate the will of God to the faithful and to deepen their knowledge of him. The translation of scripture should be a help in that process. Part of an officiant's (or celebrant's) function is to determine, as well as possible, how that knowledge of God and of his will can best be communicated. In a real sense, one is given the tools and the responsibility of choosing among them.

APPENDIX III

Basic Lore

There are some matters of custom unrelated to the basic task of the lay minister, about which information might be helpful. These include questions of liturgical colors, candles, and the like. Note that this is listed as "lore." That means that there are no rules, only traditions of varied extent.

As noted earlier, there are "green" and special seasons. Most calendars will show the Sundays after Epiphany and the Sundays after Pentecost in green. If they have explanations, they will say that green is the color of hope. It is often pointed out that the arrival of spring is heralded by the greening of the grass, the popping of green buds on bushes and trees, the spears of green leaves on crocus and tulip. It is these marks of the arrival of spring that give hope after the cold grip of winter. It is noted that it is especially appropriate that the color most often associated with worship should symbolize hope, for our faith leads us to live in hope of our salvation and in hope for the fulfillment of our lives and aspirations in the Kingdom.

The festal color is white. It is said to symbolize joy. In scripture, it is the color associated with the garments of the transfigured Jesus, as well as the raiment of the angels at the empty tomb. It is also the color of the garments of those who have been called to the Kingdom and have "washed their garments and made them white in the blood of the Lamb," as the Book of Revelation says. It is the color of purity of the divine, unbesmirched by or washed clean of the impurity of this world. It is used on all festivals and for saints who are not martyrs.

In the preparatory seasons, there are two concurrent traditions. Many use violet for Advent and Lent. It is said to be the color of penitence. Its use in both seasons, then, tends to underline their likenesses. The alternate color choices tend to emphasize the differences between the two seasons. In the old English use, blue is used during Advent. The shade is usually a "royal" blue, to emphasize the Church's expectation of a King who will return in triumph. For Lent, this use provides a "natural" or sackcloth color, usually rough woven, and often including some burlap. During Holy Week a maroon "blood" red is used, often with black. In either case, the crosses and statues in the Church are veiled during Holy Week. From Palm Sunday through Wednesday, the veiling should match the color on the altar and paraments. On Thursday, it is white. On Good Friday, it is traditionally black. The sackcloth is the biblical material for penitence and fasting. "Sackcloth and ashes" is the biblical phrase. The maroon is meant to symbolize the blood poured out for our salvation. The altar is in white for the institution of the Lord's Supper on Thursday and in black for mourning on Good Friday.

Pentecost is ordinarily celebrated in bright red to symbolize the flames that came down upon the Apostles when the Spirit was outpoured. If there is a traditional symbol for the feast, it is the dove. The Holy Week red of the old English usage is not appropriate for Pentecost. The dark red should be used for Holy Week and martyrs.

While local customs about candles vary, there are certain guidelines which might be helpful. The first is that almost everything in the Church started for a practical reason and was given a symbolic religious interpretation later. So also with candles. They exist to give light in dark buildings. The candles on the altar are for altar services. Neither the Office nor the ministry of the Word is an altar service. Hence, the two candles on the altar are inappropriate. If it is customary to have candles either behind the altar, or on the pavement at the foot of the altar, or near the lectern or pulpit, it is appropriate to light them.

There are many "rules" about lighting and extinguishing candles. The usual custom is to light the right side first, the left side second. It is customary to extinguish them in reverse order, so that the "Gospel" candle never burns alone. There is no particular reason, and if one forgets, or if the local customs vary, the matter is not of significance.

In some parishes it is customary to have a "choir prayer" said aloud before and after the service. Since each liturgy is carefully designed to have its own beginning and ending, there is good reason to eliminate such a custom.

As a simple guideline: any ceremony connected with the liturgy should underline, not distract from, the rite itself. In St. Paul's words, "Let everything be done decently and in order."

We have, from the beginning of this study until now, tried to clarify the choices a lay minister must make in fulfilling the role he or she is licensed for. No one book can answer all questions. There will be things that one as a lay minister will need to know. Don't hesitate to ask the bishop or a neighboring priest if help is needed.

The Catechism in the BCP, on p. 857, defines corporate worship in this way: "In corporate worship, we unite ourselves with others to acknowledge the holiness of God, to hear God's Word, to offer prayer, and to celebrate the sacraments." By an act of prevenient grace, each lay minister has been called to a ministry within the corporate worship of the Church. As the ministry has been received by grace, it will be fulfilled by grace. Aids and handbooks may help. Good advice may help. Preparation is necessary. Prayer, deep and sincere, for God's ever present grace is essential. By that prayer and in that grace, God bless us all who seek to serve Him in the ministry of worship.

APPENDIX IV

Church Canons Relevant to Lay Ministers

TITLE III

CANON 3.
Of Licensed Lay Persons

To be licensed by the Bishop. Sec. 1 (a). A confirmed adult communicant in goc standing may serve as Lay Reader, Pastoral Lead Lay Preacher, Lay Eucharistic Minister, or Catechi if licensed by the Bishop or Ecclesiastical Authori of the Diocese in which the person is a memb Guidelines for training and selection of such perso shall be established by the Bishop.

(b). The Presiding Bishop or the Suffragan Bishc for the Armed Forces may license a member of th Armed Forces to exercise one or more of these mii istries in the Armed Forces in accordance with th provisions of this Canon.

(c). A Diocesan Bishop or the Ecclesiastical Authorit) may license duly certified Church Army Evangelist: to exercise one or more of these ministries in accor- dance with the provisions of this Canon.

Time limit and renewal of license. Sec. 2 (a). A license shall be given only at the request, and upon the recommendation, of the Member of the Clergy in charge of the Congregation in which the person will be serving. The license shall be issued for a period of time not to exceed three years and shall be revocable by the Bishop, or upon the request of the Member of the Clergy in charge of the Con- gregation.

(b). Renewal of the license shall be determined on the basis of the acceptable performance of the ministry by the licensee and upon the endorsement of the Member of the Clergy in charge of the Congregation in which the person is serving.

(c). A person licensed in any Diocese under the provisions of this Canon may serve in another Congregation in the same or another Diocese at the invitation of the Member of the Clergy in charge, and with the consent of the Bishop in whose jurisdiction the service will occur.

Conduct of services: Directions and restrictions.

(d). The person licensed shall conform to the directions of the Bishop and the Member of the Clergy in charge of the Congregation in which the person is serving, in all matters relating to the conduct of services, the sermons to be read, and the dress to be worn. In every respect, the person licensed shall conform to the requirements and limitations set forth in the rubrics and other directions of the Book of Common Prayer.

Pastoral Leader.

Sec. 3. A Pastoral Leader is a Lay Person licensed to exercise pastoral or administrative responsibility in a Congregation under special circumstances and may be licensed to lead regularly the Offices authorized by the Book of Common Prayer. Prior to licensing, a Pastoral Leader shall be trained, examined, and found competent in the following subjects:

(a) The Holy Scriptures, contents and background;
(b) The Book of Common Prayer and The Hymnal;
(c) The conduct of public worship;
(d) Use of the voice;
(e) Church History;
(f) The Church's Doctrine as set forth in the Creeds and An Outline of the Faith, commonly called the Catechism;
(g) Parish Administration;

(h) Appropriate Canons;
(i)   Pastoral Care.

A Pastoral Leader shall not be licensed if, in the judgment of the Bishop or Ecclesiastical Authority, the Congregation is able to and has had reasonable opportunity to secure a resident Member of the Clergy in charge.

Lay Preacher.   Sec. 4. A Lay Preacher is a person licensed to preach. Prior to licensing, the Lay Preacher shall be trained, examined, and found competent in the following subjects:

(a) The Holy Scriptures, contents and background;
(b) The Book of Common Prayer and The Hymnal;
(c) The conduct of public worship;
(d) Use of the voice;
(e) Church History;
(f)   Christian Ethics and Moral Theology;
(g) The Church's Doctrine as set forth in the Creeds and An Outline of the Faith, commonly called the Catechism;
(h) Appropriate Canons;
(i)   Pastoral Care;
(j)   Homiletics.

Persons so licensed shall only preach in congregations upon the initiative and under the supervision of the Member of the Clergy in charge.

Lay Eucharistic Minister.   Sec. 5 (a). A Lay Eucharistic Minister is a person licensed to this extraordinary ministry. The Lay Eucharistic Minister shall have one or both of the following functions, as specified in the license:

(1) Administering the elements at any Celebration of Holy Eucharist in the absence of a sufficient number of Priests or Deacons assisting the celebrant;

(2) Directly following a Celebration of the Holy Eucharist on Sunday or other Principal Celebrations,

taking the Sacrament consecrated at the Celebration to members of the Congregation who, by reason of illness or infirmity, were unable to be present at the Celebration. Persons so licensed may also be known as "Lay Eucharistic Visitors."

Qualifications, requirements, and guidelines. (b). Qualifications, requirements, and guidelines for the selection, training, and use of Lay Eucharistic Ministers shall be established by the Bishop.

Not to take place of ministry of Priests and Deacons. (c). This ministry is not to take the place of the ministry of Priests and Deacons in the exercise of their office, including regular visitation of members unable to attend the Celebration of the Holy Eucharist. A Lay Eucharistic Minister should normally be under the direction of a Deacon of the Congregation, if there be one.

Catechist. Sec. 6. A Catechist is a person licensed to prepare persons for Baptism, Confirmation, Reception, and the Reaffirmation of Baptismal Vows. Prior to licensing, Catechists shall be trained, examined and found competent in the following subjects:

(a) The Holy Scriptures, contents and background;
(b) The Book of Common Prayer and The Hymnal;
(c) Church History;
(d) The Church's Doctrine as set forth in the Creeds and An Outline of the Faith, commonly called the Catechism;
(e) Methods of Catechesis.

Lay Reader. Sec. 7. A Lay Reader is a person who regularly leads public worship under the direction of a Member of the Clergy in charge of the Congregation. Training and licensing shall be under the authority of the Bishop for those persons recommended by the Member of the Clergy in charge of the Congregation, as provided by the Canons of the Diocese.

Lector. Sec. 8. A Lector is a person trained in reading of the

Word and appointed without license by the Member of the Clergy in charge of the Congregation to read lessons or lead the Prayers of the People.

TITLE I

CANON 17.

Of Regulations Respecting the Laity

Members.

Sec. 1 (d) Any person who is baptized in this Church as an adult and receives the laying on of hands by the Bishop at Baptism is to be considered, for the purpose of this and all other Canons, as both baptized and confirmed; also,

Any person who is baptized in this Church as an adult and at some time after the Baptism receives the laying on of hands by the Bishop in Reaffirmation of Baptismal Vows is to be considered, for the purpose of this and all other Canons, as both baptized and confirmed; also,

Any baptized person who received the laying on of hands at Confirmation (by any Bishop in apostolic succession) and is received into the Episcopal Church by a Bishop of this Church is to be considered, for the purpose of this and all other Canons, as both baptized and confirmed; and also,

Any baptized person who received the laying on of hands by a Bishop of this Church at Confirmation or Reception is to be considered, for the purpose of this and all other Canons, as both baptized and confirmed.

Communicants.

Sec. 2 (a) All members of this Church who have received Holy Communion in this Church at least three times during the preceding year are to be considered communicants of this Church.

(b) For the purposes of statistical consistency throughout the Church, communicants sixteen years of age and over are to be considered adult communicants.

Communicants
in good standing.

Sec. 3. All communicants of this Church who for
the previous year have been faithful in corporate
worship, unless for good cause prevented, and have
been faithful in working, praying, and giving for
the spread of the Kingdom of God, are to be
considered communicants in good standing.

A BIBLIOGRAPHY
FOR LAY MINISTERS

On the next few pages are listed books covering several subjects in which a lay minister should be fairly well-versed. The bibliography is divided into four sections: *Bible* (covering both the standard reference works and a number of other valuable resources and commentaries), *Worship and Prayer*, *Church History*, and *Doctrine*. Titles mentioned are usually standard works in the field, and most should be available through any well-stocked Christian bookstore.

A number of the books included in these lists are now out of print. Their importance, however, is by no means diminished, and a search of your local church or town library should unearth most of them. If this is unsuccessful, it is at least likely that your parish priest, or someone in his or her acquaintance, has access to a privately owned copy. The out-of-print titles are marked by an asterisk (*).

A few of the books listed were never published in this country. Again, your local bookstore should have little trouble locating or special-ordering these, or your parish priest may be of assistance. Such English titles are marked with a dagger (†).

Bibliographical information given is that which appears on the title and copyright pages of the most recent edition.

BIBLE

In addition to the various English versions of the Bible that are authorized to be read in worship (*see* p. 65), there are several books about the Bible and reference works that might prove helpful.

REFERENCE WORKS:

Albright, William F., and David N. Freedman, eds. *The Anchor Bible.* 44 vols. Garden City, N.Y.: Doubleday, 1962-.

Borsch, Frederick H., ed. *Anglicanism and the Bible.* Harrisburg, PA: Morehouse Publishing, 1984.

Buttrick, George A., ed. *The Interpreter's Bible,* (12 vol.). Nashville, Tennessee: Abingdon Press, 1951-1957.

_____, and Keith R. Crim, eds. *The Interpreter's Dictionary of the Bible.* (5 vols.). Nashville, Tennessee: Abingdon Press, 1980.

Keck, Leander, ed. *The New Interpreter's Bible,* Vol. I. Nashville, Tennessee: Abingdon Press, 1994.

May, Herbert G., ed. *The Oxford Bible Atlas.* London: Oxford University Press, 1985.

*_____, and Bruce M. Metzger, eds. *The New Oxford Annotated Bible, with the Apocryphia* (RSV) Rev. ed. New York: Oxford University Press, 1977.

Richardson, Alan, ed. *A Theological Word Book of the Bible.* New York: Macmillan, 1962.

Sandmel, Samuel, ed. *Oxford Study Edition: The New English Bible, with the Apocrypha.* New York: Oxford University Press, 1976.

Throckmorton, Burton H., ed. *Gospel Parallels: A Sypnosis of the First Three Gospels.* 4th ed. New York: Thomas Nelson, 1979.

Wright, George E., and Floyd V. Filson. *Westminster Historical Maps of Bible Lands.* Philadelphia: The Westminster Press, 1956.

OTHER RESOURCE WORKS:

Bennett, Robert A., and O. C. Edwards. *The Bible for Today's Church*. Church's Teaching Ser. Vol. 2. New York and San Francisco: Harper & Row, 1979.

Fuller, Reginald H. *The New Testament in Current Study.* New York: Charles Scribner's, 1976.

_____. *Preaching the New Lectionary: The Word of God for the Church Today*. Collegeville, Minnesota: The Liturgical Press, 1984.

Kubo, Sakae, and Walter Specht. *So Many Versions?: Twentieth Century English Versions of the Bible*. Grand Rapids, Michigan: Zondervan, 1983.

Napier, Davie. *Song of the Vineyard: A Guide Through the Old Testament*. Philadelphia: Fortress Press, 1981.

Sayers, Dorothy L. *The Man Born to Be King.* North Pomfret, Vermont: David and Charles, 1983.

Sydnor, William. *Introductions to the Scripture Read in Worship*. Harrisburg, PA: Morehouse Publishing, 1991.

WORSHIP AND PRAYER

The Hymnal 1982, New York: The Church Hymnal Corp.

The Hymnal 1982 Companion. New York: The Church Hymnal Corp., 1990.

Borsch, Frederick H. *Introducing the Lessons of the Church Year; A Guide for Lay Readers and Congregations*. Valley Forge, PA: Trinity Press International, 19.

Stuhlman, Byron D. *Prayer Book Rubrics Expanded*. New York: Church Hymnal Corp., 1987.

Dix, Dom Gregory. *The Shape of the Liturgy*. New York and San Francisco: Harper & Row, 1982.

Edwards, Dan Thomas. *A Study Guide to Prayer Book Spirituality*. New York: Church Hymnal Corp., 1990.

Hatchett, Marion J. *Commentary on the American Prayer Book.* New York and San Francisco: Harper & Row, 1981.

_____. *A Guide to the Practice of Church Music.* New York: The Church Hymnal Corp., 1989.

Jungmann, Josef A., S. J. *The Mass: An Historical, Theological and Pastoral Survey.* Collegeville, Minnesota: The Liturgical Press, 1976.

_____. *The Mass of the Roman Rite.* 2 vols. Westminster, Maryland: Christian Classics, 1986.

†Milner-White, Eric. *My God and My Glory.* London: S.P.C.K., 1954.

†_____. *A Procession Passion of Prayers.* London: S.P.C.K., 1950.

Mitchell, Leonel. *Praying Shapes Believing: A Theological Commentary on the Book of Common Prayer.* Harrisburg, PA: Morehouse Publishing, 1990.

O'Driscoll, Herbert. *A Year of the Lord.* Harrisburg, PA: Morehouse Publishing, 1987.

Price, Charles P., and Louis Weil. *Liturgy for Living.* Church's Teaching Ser. Vol. 5. New York and San Francisco: Harper & Row, 1979.

Shepherd, Massey H., Jr. *The Oxford American Prayer Book Commentary.* New York: Oxford University Press, 1950.

*_____. *The Psalms in Christian Worship: A Practical Guide.* Collegeville, Minnesota: The Liturgical Press, 1976.

Suter, John Wallace, ed. *The Book of English Collects.* New York: Harper & Row, 1940.

*Thornton, Martin. *Christian Proficiency.* New York: Morehouse-Barlow, 1959.

Treasures from the Spiritual Classics series. Compiled by Roger L. Roberts. 8 vols. Harrisburg, PA: Morehouse Publishing, 1982.

Underhill, Evelyn. *The Spiritual Life.* Harrisburg, PA: Morehouse Publishing, 1984.
Wright, J. Robert. *Prayer Book Spirituality.* New York: Church Hymnal Corp., 1989.

CHURCH HISTORY

*Addison, James T. *The Episcopal Church in the United States, 1789-1931.* Reprint. Hamden, Connecticut: Shoe String Press, 1969.
*Albright, Raymond W. *A History of the Protestant Episcopal Church.* New York: Macmillan, 1964.
Booty, John E. *The Church in History.* Church's Teaching Ser. Vol. 3. New York and San Francisco: Harper & Row, 1979.
_____. *What Makes Us Episcopalians?* Harrisburg, PA: Morehouse Publishing, 1982.
Cross, Frank L., and Elizabeth A. Livingstone, eds. *The Oxford Dictionary of the Christian Church.* Rev. ed. New York: Oxford University Press, 1984.
Marty, Martin E. *A Short History of Christianity.* Philadelphia: Fortress Press, 1980.
Moorman, J. R. H. *A History of the Church in England.* Harrisburg, PA: Morehouse Publishing, 1980.
Prichard, Robert W. *A History of the Episcopal Church.* Harrisburg, PA: Morehouse Publishing, 1991.
Prichard, Robert W., ed. *Readings from the History of the Episcopal Church.* Harrisburg, PA: Morehouse Publishing, 1986.
*Spencer, Bonnell, O.H.C. *Ye are the Body.* Rev. ed. West Park, New York: Holy Cross Publications, 1965.
Sumner, David E. *The Episcopal Church's History, 1945-1985.* Harrisburg, PA: Morehouse Publishing, 1987.
Walker, Williston. *The History of the Christian Church,* 4th ed. R. T. Handy, editor. New York: Charles Scribner's, 1985.

84   *A Lay Minister's Guide*

Williams, Charles. *The Descent of the Dove*. Grand Rapids,
    Michigan: William B. Eerdmans, 1965.
*Wilson, Frank E. *The Divine Commission*. 5th ed. New York:
    Morehouse-Barlow, 1963.

DOCTRINE

Atwater, George P. *The Episcopal Church: Its Message for
    Today*. Rev. ed. Harrisburg, PA: Morehouse Publishing,
    1978.
†Doctrine Commission of the Church of England. *Christian
    Believing: The Nature of the Christian Faith and its
    Expression in Holy Scripture and Creeds*. London:
    S.P.C.K., 1976.
Ferguson, Franklin C. *A Pilgrimage in Faith: An Introduction
    to the Episcopal Church*. Harrisburg, PA: Morehouse
    Publishing, 1979.
Gray, William and Betty. *The Episcopal Church Welcomes
    You: An Introduction to Its History, Worship and Mission*.
    New York and San Francisco: Harper & Row, 1974.
Holmes, Urban T. *What Is Anglicanism?* Harrisburg, PA:
    Morehouse Publishing, 1982.
Micks, Marianne H. *Introduction to Theology*. Rev. ed.
    New York and San Francisco: Harper & Row, 1983.
*Moss, C. B. *The Christian Faith: An Introduction to Dogmatic
    Theology*. New York: Morehouse-Gorham, 1954.
Norris, Richard A. *Understanding the Faith of the Church*.
    Church's Teaching Ser. Vol. 4. New York and San
    Francisco: Harper & Row, 1979.
†Quick, Oliver. *The Doctrines of the Creed*. London: Nisbet &
    Co., Ltd., 1949.
*Ramsey, Arthur Michael. *Introducing the Christian Faith*.
    New York: Morehouse-Barlow, 1970.
*Sayers, Dorothy. *A Matter of Eternity*. Rosamond K. Sprague,

editor. Grand Rapids, Michigan: William B. Eerdmans, 1973.

*Shideler, Mary. *Creed for a Christian Sceptic.* Grand Rapids, Michigan: William B. Eerdmans, 1968.

†Temple, William. *About Christ.* London: S.C.M. Press, 1962.

*Terwilliger, Robert E. *Christian Believing.* Wilton, Connecticut: Morehouse-Barlow, 1973.

Wilson, Frank E. *Faith and Practice.* Rev. ed. Harrisburg, PA: Morehouse Publishing, 1981.

Another essential is the text of the Church's standard lay readers' training course:

*Partridge, Edmund B. *The Church in Perspective: Standard Course for Lay Readers.* 2d ed. Wilton, Connecticut: Morehouse-Barlow, 1976.

LAY EUCHARISTIC MINISTERS

Ely, Beth. *A Manual for Lay Eucharistic Ministers.* Harrisburg, PA: Morehouse Publishing, 1991.

Gulick, Anna D. *This Bread, This Cup: An Introduction to the Eucharist.* Harrisburg, PA: Morehouse Publishing, 1992.

LECTORS

Kryszck, Stell A. *Training for Lectors.* Indianapolis: St. Paul's Episcopal Church, 1986.

Mulligan, Frank. *Lector's Guide to the Episcopal Eucharistic Lectionary.* New York, N.Y.: St. Mark's Press, 1987.

Scott-Craig, T.S.K. *A Guide to Pronouncing Biblical Names.* Harrisburg, PA: Morehouse Publishing, 1982.

Sydnor, William. *Introductions to the Scripture Read in Worship.* Harrisburg, PA: Morehouse Publishing, 1991.

_____. *Your Voice, God's Word.* Harrisburg, PA: Morehouse Publishing, 1988.

LITURGICAL PLANNING

Howard, Thomas. *The Liturgy Explained.* Harrisburg, PA: Morehouse Publishing, 1981.

Mitchell, Leonel. *Planning the Church Year.* Harrisburg, PA: Morehouse Publishing, 1991.

Russell, Joseph P. *The Daily Lectionary—Year One.* 2 vols. *Year Two.* 2 vols. Cincinnati: Forward Movement, n.d.

Stevick, Daniel B. *The Crafting of Liturgy.* New York: Church Hymnal Corp., 1990.

TOTAL MINISTRY

Pittenger, Norman. *The Ministry of All Christians.* Harrisburg, PA: Morehouse Publishing, 1983.

Rowthorn, Anne. *The Liberation of the Laity.* Harrisburg, PA: Morehouse Publishing, 1986.

www.ingramcontent.com/pod-product-compliance
Lightning Source LLC
Jackson TN
JSHW081332130125
77033JS00014B/526